FINDING GOD
IN THE LAND OF
NARNIA

FINDING GOD
IN THE LAND OF

KURT BRUNER
JIM WARE

SALT**RIVER**™

AN IMPRINT OF TYNDALE HOUSE PUBLISHERS, INC.

Visit Tyndale's exciting Web site at www.tyndale.com

TYNDALE is a registered trademark of Tyndale House Publishers, Inc.

SaltRiver and the *SaltRiver* logo are trademarks of Tyndale House Publishers, Inc.

Finding God in the Land of Narnia

Designed by Luke Daab

Library of Congress Cataloging-in-Publication Data

Bruner, Kurt D.
   Finding God in the land of Narnia / Kurt Bruner, Jim Ware.
      p. cm.
Includes bibliographical references.
   ISBN 0-8423-8104-X (hc)
   1. Lewis, C. S. (Clive Staples), 1898-1963. Chronicles of Narnia. 2. Children's stories, English—History and criticism. 3. Christian fiction, English—History and criticism. 4. Fantasy fiction, English—History and criticism. 5. Spiritual life in literature. 6. Narnia (Imaginary place) 7. God in literature. I. Ware, Jim. II. Title.
PR6023.E926C5323 2004
823'.912—dc22   2003024945

Printed in the United States of America

09   08   07   06   05
6   5   4   3   2   I

Dedication
To Shaun, who can hardly wait to see real Narnia,
and to Ian, who is headed Further Up and Further In

Table of Contents

Introduction

They say that one test of egocentricity is asking yourself how many people need to look good in a group photo for you to like the picture. I guess I'm egocentric. That's why I was so disappointed with a particular snapshot taken during our 1999 trip to England. My wife, Olivia, looks fantastic. I look like a nerd. So I thought it belonged in the discard pile—until something caught my eye in the top left corner, making it one of my most cherished photographs.

While on a business trip to London, I took a day to visit a little pub in Oxford known as the Eagle and Child, where several writers who called themselves the Inklings routinely gathered six decades earlier to hear and critique bits of one another's work. For years I had imagined what it would have been like to sit in a quaint English pub eavesdropping on conversations between two of my literary heroes, J. R. R. Tolkien, creator of Middle-earth, and C. S. Lewis, the man who conceived the land of Narnia. Fifty-plus years later, the closest I could get was to visit the spot—perhaps even share the same booth—where two of the twentieth century's most brilliant Christian writers once sat.

I don't know what I expected—perhaps a shrine marking the place where these great men once gathered, or a gallery celebrating their legacy, or a reading room filled with their books. What I found was something else entirely. The pub was nothing more than, well, a pub. People—mostly college students—were sitting around eating, drinking, smoking, and talking. As far as I could tell, not a soul was treating the place with due reverence. Not one person seemed to be reflecting upon the spiritual themes within the works of Tolkien, Lewis, or any other Tom, Dick, or Harry. And so, disappointed by the ordinariness of the place, unable to locate a table "in memory of" my literary heroes, I asked someone to take a quick snapshot of us before we left.

Weeks later, back home, my wife and I were flipping through photo memories of our trip. That was when I noticed that in the top left corner of the picture in which Olivia looks great and I look like a nerd is the bottom half of a portrait. It seems that just above the booth in which we sat for our snapshot hangs a picture of C. S. Lewis! The room was too dark and the smoke too thick to notice while we were there, but the camera flash revealed that we were, apparently, sitting in the very place Lewis and Tolkien once sat. I now tell friends that I went to Oxford and had my picture taken with the man who penned *The Chronicles of Narnia*—the man, incidentally, who has done more to inspire my faith than any other.

Awakenings

C. S. Lewis, Jack to his friends, is known today as the Oxford don who became a great apologist for the Christian faith. But it was not always so. In fact, he went to Oxford as a skeptic, seeing the Christian gospel as just another myth bringing comfort to the weak-minded—offering little to the more sophisticated intellect.

"I believe in no religion," seventeen-year-old Jack wrote to a friend. "There is absolutely no proof for any of them, and from a philosophical standpoint, Christianity is not even the best."[1] By the time he was thirty-two, however, he had a very different view, as expressed in a note to that same friend: "Christianity is God expressing Himself through what we call 'real things,' . . . namely the actual incarnation, crucifixion, and resurrection."[2]

What made the change in Lewis? In a word, fantasy. It is no stretch to say that Lewis's faith journey began as a result of reading stories that were dripping with Christian truth—awakening within him a desire for something he didn't possess. Like the wonderful aroma of home-baked cookies invading his nostrils, these stories gave Jack a whiff of joy, making him hungry for the full reality of its source.

In later life, Lewis would credit the author of those stories, nineteenth-century minister George MacDonald, with having influenced virtually every word he ever wrote—including Narnia. It began with *Phantastes,* a dream-like tale in which a boy wished to visit fairy-country. He woke the next morning in an enchanted wood where he encountered profound happiness mixed with perilous adventure, including death and rebirth of sorts. At first, Lewis didn't recognize the story or the desire it stirred in him to be Christian. Only later, after having found the aroma's source, did Lewis realize what had occurred. Lewis said he "crossed a great frontier" while reading *Phantastes* that placed him on a quest for joy. This pursuit eventually found its source in the same God of Christianity he had abandoned in childhood.[3] And so, thanks to the imagination of George MacDonald, C. S. Lewis found his way home—and was met by a plate of warm cookies.

I had a similar experience while sitting in a London recording studio. As executive producer for a radio dramatization of *The Chronicles of Narnia,* I was privileged to work with an extremely talented group of writers, producers, and actors as they brought these seven wonderful stories to life. With my eyes closed, I listened to voices from behind the glass as the theater of my mind entered into the drama. Each encounter with the great Lion Aslan brought a shiver down my spine and a lump to my throat. It was like encountering something—no, Some*one*—more frightening, yet more comforting than any I had ever met before. I found myself moved in ways decades of church attendance and religious instruction had never accomplished. I was catching a whiff of something much more joyous than I knew.

Months later, my nine-year-old son got his own shivers. Our entire family was driving in the car listening to the final production of *The Lion, the Witch and the Wardrobe.* Not a word was spoken as we endured the dreadful scene of Aslan's death on the stone table. A deep sadness rested upon Shaun as he absorbed the injustice and loss. But then, moments later, he was overwhelmed with celebration as he discovered that Aslan was alive again. The gloom of death overtaken by the delight of resurrection, Shaun could not contain his excitement. "That's just like Jesus!" he screamed from the backseat.

Like most kids raised in Sunday school, Shaun had heard the story of Jesus' death and resurrection literally dozens of times. It had become routine, expected—perhaps even boring. But through a fantasy tale that had none of what Lewis called "stained glass and Sunday school associations," Shaun was caught off guard, surprised by the most wonderful and potent truth of Christian faith. The effect on his heart, like my own sitting in that studio, was a whiff of true delight. We entered into the experience of the gospel rather than merely exploring its tenets. And along the way, we "crossed a great frontier" that awakened a new, more vibrant faith.

KURT BRUNER AND JIM WARE

Another World

What George MacDonald did for the faith and imagination of C. S. Lewis, Lewis has done for millions who enjoy his fantasy tales. With combined sales of more than eighty-five million copies and as the inspiration behind the feature film, the seven *Chronicles of Narnia* books are more popular than ever. And with good reason. With the possible exception of J. R. R. Tolkien, no twentieth-century writer more masterfully married the enchantment of fantasy with the enrichment of faith. The Narnia stories are like a meal with the nourishment of meat and vegetables but the taste of cake and candy. Both the dreams of fairyland and the promise of heaven invade the imagination at the same time, baptizing it with wonderful and unexpected effects.

The problem, of course, is that we rarely associate pleasure with nourishment. The Narnia tales are such good children's stories, we resist the notion that they allegorize the gospel story. Lewis himself debunked the idea that his tales are mere Christian allegory, explaining that the Christian truths pushed their way into the story on their own. His theology was part of him, so it became part of what he created—like air bubbling to the water's surface:

Some people seem to think that I began by asking myself how I could say something about Christianity to children; then fixed on the fairy tale as an instrument; then collected information about child-psychology and decided what age group I'd write for; then drew up a list of basic Christian truths and hammered out "allegories" to embody them. This is all pure moonshine. I couldn't write in that way at all. Everything began with images; a faun carrying an umbrella, a queen on a sledge, a magnificent lion. At first there wasn't anything Christian about them; that element pushed itself in of its own accord. It was part of the bubbling.[4]

The Narnia stories are not allegory. Rather they grow out of a central supposition. Suppose there existed another world peopled by animals rather than human beings. Suppose that world fell, like ours, and had in it someone the equivalent of Christ.

Aslan entered Narnia in the form of a lion just as Jesus came into this world in the form of a man. Based upon this supposition, Lewis created a fantasy world that depicts the central theme of our real world—redemption through the incarnate God's death and resurrection. The magical part is that this mythical Christ somehow draws us ever deeper to the Real.

In May of 1955, the mother of a nine-year-old boy named Laurence wrote to C. S. Lewis, explaining that Laurence was concerned that he loved Aslan more than Jesus. To her delighted surprise, she received a reply ten days later that included the following:

> Laurence can't really love Aslan more than Jesus, even if he feels that's what he is doing. For the things he loves Aslan for doing or saying are simply the things Jesus really did and said. So that when Laurence thinks he is loving Aslan, he is really loving Jesus: and perhaps loving Him more than he ever did before.[5]

Another Name

There is no doubt that C. S. Lewis hoped his Narnia tales would draw readers toward a deeper love of Jesus. In fact, none other than Aslan himself tells us so. At the conclusion of *Voyage of the "Dawn Treader,"* Lucy and Edmund encountered a lamb inviting the children to share breakfast. Hoping to see the great Lion, Lucy asked the Lamb whether they were on the path to Aslan's country. "Not for you," replied the Lamb. "For you the door into Aslan's country is from your own world."

Edmund expressed shock, surprised to hear that there might be a way into Aslan's country from his own world. So he asked the Lamb if such a way existed, thrilled by the possibility yet cautious—worried that he might have misunderstood.

Suddenly, the gentle lamb transfigured into the great Lion. "There is a way into my country from all the worlds."

It was Aslan himself. The joyous embrace of reunion quickly dissolved into sad realization that it was time for Lucy and Edmund to leave Narnia and go home. Eager to know when they might get to come back, hoping it would be very soon, Lucy learned that she would never return. She was too old and must begin to draw close to her own world. And while she would miss Narnia, her real sorrow was the thought of never meeting Aslan again.

"But you shall meet me, dear one," he reassured. "But there I have another name. You must learn to know me by that name. This was the very reason why you were brought to Narnia, that by knowing me here for a little, you may know me better there."[6]

The same is true for us. Lewis draws us into another world so that we might experience Christ by another name. And when we return home from the adventure, we bring with us a better understanding and deeper love for the Savior. Or at the very least, we return having smelled the aroma of joy—and craving its true source.

In June of 1953, an eleven-year-old girl named Hila had just such an awakening while reading the Narnia stories—an experience she later described as "an indefinable stirring and longing." She wrote to C. S. Lewis, inquiring about this "other name" Aslan suggested. She, like Edmund, wanted to know the way into Aslan's country from our world. Lewis replied:

> As to Aslan's other name, well I want you to guess. Has there never been anyone in this world who (1.) Arrived at the same time as Father Christmas. (2.) Said he was the son of the Great Emperor. (3.) Gave himself up for someone else's fault to be jeered at and killed by wicked people. (4.) Came to life again. . . . Don't you really know His name in this world.[7]

And so we begin our own journey into Narnia. As in our earlier book, *Finding God in The Lord of the Rings*, we will briefly touch upon specific scenes and themes from the story told before reflecting upon implications for life in the real world. It is not our intention to turn Lewis's stories into sermons. But we do hope to draw spiritual insights from the faith that inspired their author and informed their plots. We seek to enrich rather than replace the experience of reading *The Chronicles of Narnia.*

Whether you are a Narnia fan concerned you might love Aslan more than Jesus, or a cynic who needs to cross the threshold of faith, we invite you to push beyond the fur coats of this world and enter the snowy wood of imagination. The light just ahead is much more than a mere lamp-post. It is the light of God millions have discovered in the land of Narnia.

In the darkness something was happening at last. A voice had begun to sing.

—*THE MAGICIAN'S NEPHEW*, CHAPTER 8,
"THE FIGHT AT THE LAMP-POST"

ASLAN'S SONG

❋

It was pitch-black. Not one of the six could see a thing. Frank, the Cabby, assumed they had accidentally fallen into an open manhole over subway construction. A reasonable guess, since the last thing he recalled was running down the street chasing a tall woman in white who was atop his stolen horse. There was some commotion involving two young children and an older gentleman, and then sudden blackout. Not a trace of light could be detected. Eyes open or shut made no difference. They were enveloped by complete and utter darkness.

The children, Polly and Digory, had a different idea. Using the magic rings to enter the Wood between the Worlds, they had intended to get the White Witch back to her home, the dreaded land of Charn. They hadn't intended to bring Uncle Andrew, or the Cabby, or his horse. But anyone touching a person wearing the rings magically goes along.

"Perhaps this is Charn," suggested Digory, thinking they'd arrived in the middle of the night. But the Witch knew better. It was not Charn. They had entered the wrong pool, bringing them into an empty world—a world not yet formed. Nothingness.

Uncle Andrew, the magician who got them into this mess to begin with by meddling with dark arts and magic rings, cowardly whispered to Digory that the two of them should use the rings to return home at once, leaving the others behind. Digory resisted, unwilling to abandon Polly or the other innocent bystanders. As Andrew chastised the boy, they were suddenly hushed.

Something was happening. The silent darkness had been invaded by something, distant and slight at first, but gradually rising. It was music, a lovely song performed by a singular voice. Then other voices joined—as if beauty, strength, and awe were approaching the frightened band to overtake their stifling emptiness with vibrant life.

And then, on cue with the latter voices, the black sky exploded with the blazing light of stars—performing in response to and in harmony with the First Voice. After that, colors emerged from the horizon, again following the melodic instructions of the song, and a brilliant, newborn sun arose. To Polly, Digory, and Frank, these were moments of pure bliss, like diving into a cool, refreshing pool on a hot summer's day. But to the Witch and Uncle Andrew, they were terrible—prompting an ominous dread rather than an unspeakable joy.

The chorus continued, spawning hills and valleys, rocks and rivers—all bursting forth as if seedlings sprouting from the garden of what would become a much larger world teeming with life.

And then he appeared, the First Voice from whose mouth the great song bellowed. It was a huge, shaggy Lion, facing the sun and seeming to empower its illumination. He altered the music, as if a new movement in a symphony had begun. It had, inviting grass, trees, frogs, panthers, beavers, mice, birds, Fauns, Dwarfs, and all forms of living creatures to blossom into being.

Finally, to the shock and thrill of the watching children, the great Lion spoke: "Narnia, awake." It was a command mixed with invitation, the form of life receiving the breath of life. His words were like a conductor's dropping baton. It was time for the music he had placed before them to be performed.

* * * * *

"And it came to pass," begins the mythology behind Tolkien's Middle-earth, "that Ilúvatar called together all the

Ainur and declared to them a mighty theme, unfolding to them things greater and more wonderful than he had yet revealed. . . . 'Of the theme that I have declared to you, I will now that ye make in harmony together a Great Music. . . . But I will sit and hearken, and be glad that through you great beauty has been wakened into song.' "

Narnia is not the first world to begin with a creation song. Decades before C. S. Lewis published his first Narnia tale, close friend and spiritual mentor J. R. R. Tolkien penned *The Silmarillion,* a creation myth for a world whose inhabitants would be Hobbits, Elves, Wizards, and Dwarves. Both men loved ancient mythology, created other worlds, and shared a devotion to Christian faith. And both men drew inspiration from the story of how our real world came into being as described in Scripture.

The earth was without form, and void; and darkness was on the face of the deep. (GENESIS 1:2)

Ours was once like the dark, unformed world into which Digory, Polly, and the others fell. If it were possible to visit and experience that place, you would feel much like those falling into the wrong pool in the Wood between the Worlds. Eyes open or shut, you would sense only a silent, oppressive nothingness.

But everything would quickly change as you began to hear the first notes of a distant, building song.

Then God said, "Let there be light"; and there was light. (GENESIS 1:3)

Suddenly, as if switching on a lamp so that you could observe the rest of the music coming to life, light would dispel the darkness.

Then God said, "Let the waters under the heavens be gathered together into one place, and let the dry land appear"; and it was so. (GENESIS 1:9)

Then God said, "Let the earth bring forth grass, the herb that yields seed, and the fruit tree that yields fruit according to its kind." . . . And God saw that it was good. (GENESIS 1:11-12)

Then God said, "Let the waters abound with an abundance of living creatures, and let birds fly above the earth across the face of the firmament of the heavens." . . . Then God said, "Let the earth bring forth the living creature according to its kind: cattle and creeping thing and beast of the earth, each according to its kind"; and it was so. (GENESIS 1:20, 24)

In the yet incomplete world of Narnia, the great Lion sang—and it was so. In our forming world, God spoke—and it was so. No masterpiece can take shape without an artist. No story can be told without an author. Nothing exists but that which came from the brush and pen of God. He composed the symphony others merely echo and painted the portrait others reflect. He engineered the first architectural structures, called mountains and trees; programmed the first computer, called the brain; and invented the first miracle

5

drug, called the immune system. They all started in His imagination, an imagination that has enabled our own.

So God created man in His own image; in the image of God He created him; male and female He created them. (GENESIS 1:27)

We compose, paint, invent, write, and plan only because He did it first. Or rather, because He spoke it first. God's word, like Aslan's song, invited us into the miracle of Creation—a creation that began with Him, is sustained by Him, and will culminate in Him.

For of Him and through Him and to Him are all things, to whom be glory forever. Amen. (ROMANS 11:36)

And that is the reason our world, and our lives, can be transformed from pitch-darkness to glorious, life-giving light!

REFLECTION

God spoke, or rather sang, our world into existence.

> *"Son of Adam," said the Lion. "There is an evil witch abroad in my new land of Narnia. Tell these good Beasts how she came here."*
>
> —THE MAGICIAN'S NEPHEW, CHAPTER 11, "DIGORY AND HIS UNCLE ARE BOTH IN TROUBLE"

EVIL HAS ENTERED

※

Digory was frightened, as well he should have been. Just standing before the great Lion was enough to make one's knees knock and hands quiver. But to stand before him when he was upset at something you'd done, well, that would make the bravest grown-up tremble and weep. For some reason, however, Digory sensed he was in big trouble—but in no danger.

It had all started when Digory and Polly went looking for adventure by climbing through the attics over the row of connected houses in which they lived. Hoping to enter an empty home, they accidentally found themselves inside his uncle Andrew's study, the one strictly off-limits to children. Things happened quickly: Polly touching a yellow ring. Uncle Andrew making Digory go after her. Encountering the strange wood filled with pools. Entering Charn and discovering a motionless world with a dying sun. Finding the great hall filled with what appeared to be noblemen and ladies frozen in place like characters in a wax museum or a photograph. Noticing the grand lady in white, who must have been their queen, stationary with the rest. And the inscription under the bell and hammer:

> *Make your choice, adventurous Stranger;*
> *Strike the bell and bide the danger,*
> *Or wonder, till it drives you mad,*
> *What would have followed if you had.*

Despite Polly's warnings, the enticement was too great for Digory. He simply had to ring the bell and discover what magic might be released. That is when the real trouble began.

The tall, beautiful woman in white awoke. Queen Jadis was her name, the last queen of this dying world. Very quickly the children learned that the queen's outward loveliness did not reflect a kind heart. Just the opposite. In fact, her willingness to use what she called "the Deplorable Word" is what killed her world and all who lived there. It was her right, she said, necessary to retain power. The little people didn't matter; they existed to serve her. She was an evil person.

Things moved quickly again: Escaping Charn by putting on the rings. Unintentionally bringing the queen with them back into their own world. Uncle Andrew's surprise at meeting Jadis, and his eager effort to satisfy her royal demands. The commotion near the lamppost that brought them all into a yet unformed Narnia.

And now—only a few short hours after the great Lion created his splendid, unblemished world—Digory found himself giving an account of how evil has been allowed to invade its borders.

"This is the Boy who did it," Aslan announced to the Talking Beasts encircling him. Commanded to tell how the White Witch entered their world, Digory made a few fumbling attempts to justify his actions. But he finally admitted the temptation and his mistake. Aslan would give Digory a chance to redeem himself. But for now, the damage was done.

"You see, friends," explained Aslan, "before the new, clean world I gave you is seven hours old, a force of evil has already entered it."

*　*　*　*　*

Pouring yourself a large glass of cold milk, you look forward to enjoying it with a warm chocolate-chip cookie. But while taking a drink you discover that the milk has soured, causing you to spew it out of your mouth. A wonderful moment is ruined.

You bite into a crisp, ripe, red apple. The juice drips down your chin as you enjoy the delicious flavor. But then, at about bite four, a sudden change. Your taste buds are invaded by an unexpected bitterness. Your face contorts in re-action. Looking down at the fruit, you notice the dark form of half a worm protruding from the whiteness. You have bit-ten into an invader, spoiling the pleasure of your snack.

Our world, like Narnia, was made completely good. It was created sweet, refreshing, and clean. But something hap-pened that spoiled the milk, invaded the apple. And we've been tasting the bitter fallout ever since.

"Enemy-occupied territory," wrote C. S. Lewis in *Mere Christianity,* "that is what this world is." You see, the man who created Narnia understood that only good can create: a good God who made a good world. But evil, while unable to create, is still able to invade, to corrupt, and to spoil. And that is precisely what happened.

In Narnia, the invasion—aided by a boy's mischief—came in the person of the White Witch, the self-described Queen Jadis of Charn. After bringing death to her own world, she sought to enslave another. In our world, the inva-sion—aided by Adam's fall—came in the person of Lucifer, the highest created being of the heavenly realm. He was God's most gifted and trusted servant, described by the prophet Ezekiel as "the seal of perfection, full of wisdom and perfect in beauty" (Ezekiel 28:12). He was entrusted to protect Eden, the garden of God. But one day, everything changed. The insanity of pride entered his heart.

You were perfect in your ways from the day you were created, till iniq- uity was found in you. Your heart was lifted up because of your beauty; you corrupted your wisdom for the sake of your splendor.

(EZEKIEL 28:15, 17)

Dig below the surface of all evil and you will find that the root is pride. It is pride that demands its way, refuses to sub- mit, rebels against authority, and inflates its own sense of worth. And it is pride that drives the created one to shake his fist in the face of his Creator and demand the throne.

You said in your heart, "I will ascend to heaven; I will raise my throne above the stars of God; I will sit enthroned on the mount of assembly, on the utmost heights of the sacred mountain. I will ascend above the tops of the clouds; I will make myself like the Most High." (ISAIAH 14:13-14, NIV)

And so a good world was invaded by an evil usurper trying to assume God's rightful throne. A land made for the sweet taste of love, justice, and virtue has been soured by hate, in- jury, and vice. Lucifer was created to serve and honor God. But he rebelled. And now, the Eden he was appointed to pro- tect has become the garden he seeks to rule.

"But do not be cast down," come the words of our God through the mouth of Aslan. "Evil will come of that evil, but it is still a long way off, and I will see to it that the worst falls upon myself."[8]

Evil will one day be overthrown, because good and evil are not, as some believe, equal forces battling to the death. Evil,

11

according to the creator of Narnia, is a parasite—not the original thing. So in the long haul, only one has any real possibility of life. To quote Lewis:

> Christianity agrees with Dualism that this universe is at war. But it does not think this is a war between independent powers. It thinks it is a civil war, a rebellion, and that we are living in a part of the universe occupied by the rebel. Christianity is the story of how the rightful king has landed, you might say landed in disguise, and is calling us all to take part in a great campaign of sabotage.[9]

In the land of Narnia, evil began offstage and invaded the goodness that should rightfully rule. Digory and others, therefore, would be called upon to participate in redemption by resisting the Witch and her minions in order to restore what should be. We have the same calling, bold and courageous because our God has promised to take upon Himself the worst evil can dish out. And so we can live with the certainty that "evil will come of that evil."

REFLECTION
We live in enemy-occupied territory.

> "Oh—Aslan, sir," said Digory, turning red, "I forgot to tell you. The Witch has already eaten one of those apples."
>
> —*THE MAGICIAN'S NEPHEW*, CHAPTER 14, "THE PLANTING OF THE TREE"

ALL GET WHAT THEY WANT

✳

More than anything in the world, Digory wanted his mother well. Back home, she was sick in bed with an illness that was stealing her life. That is why Digory was eager to find something in this magical land that might provide a cure. It was a wish that nearly ruined everything.

Aslan had given Digory a chance to temporarily right the wrong of bringing the Witch into Narnia by sending him to retrieve an apple from a particular tree beyond the western mountains. The great Lion wished to plant a tree that would protect his new land for many generations. When asked to go, Digory wondered whether the Lion might give him something to cure his mother as payment for a job well done. But he held his tongue, knowing he was in no position to cut deals.

Along with Polly, Digory rode atop Fledge—the newly winged horse—to reach their destination. Upon arrival, they found an intimidating golden gate with a silver inscription. It warned that the fruit, intended for others, must not be stolen for oneself. "For those who steal or those who climb my wall," it cautioned, "shall find their heart's desire and find despair."

Digory approached the tree standing tall in the center of the garden—the one with great silver apples hanging from its lush branches. Following Aslan's instruction, he plucked one of the apples and placed it in his breast pocket. But first he took in its delicious smell. Digory's mouth began to water as his hunger intensified. He longed to taste the fruit and tried to convince himself that it would be all right. After all, he was obeying the order to bring one back for others. What possible harm could there be in eating one himself? But he stopped short after noticing a majestic bird perched atop an upper branch. In a magical land, you never knew who might be watching what you did.

Turning back toward the others, Digory was suddenly face-to-face with the Witch. Her mouth was stained with awful, dark traces of juice from an apple core she tossed aside. Frightened by the triumphantly devious look on her face, Digory fled the scene. The Witch pursued. More treacherously, she spoke, promising information that would make Digory happy. Half of him resisted. But the other half wanted to know.

He was too hasty, she suggested, bringing the untasted apple to the Lion. Didn't Digory realize what that fruit could do? "What about this Mother of yours whom you pretend to love so? Do you not see, Fool, that one bite of that apple would heal her?" Digory could disregard the Lion's errand, return to his world, and make his mother well with the magic fruit.

Such a dilemma! Digory was tempted to take the Witch's advice. After all, there was nothing he wanted more than his mother's healing. But taking the apple would be stealing. It would be disobeying the great Lion's command. Still, no one in his world needed know about it. Might the good end justify the wayward means?

No, he wouldn't do it—as much as he would have liked to. Stealing was wrong. And besides, it felt better trusting the Lion than trusting the Witch.

"I've brought you the apple you wanted, sir." Standing before Aslan, Digory was praised for a job well done. Somehow, the Lion knew that Digory was tempted to eat and tempted to take. But he had resisted. And now the full picture became clear.

The apple did indeed lead to long life. But when taken illegitimately, with an evil heart, it also led to length of misery.

"That is what happens to those who pluck and eat fruits at the wrong time and in the wrong way," Aslan explained. "The fruit is good, but they loathe it ever after. All get what they want; they do not always like it."

Digory, relieved that he had not listened to the Witch, understood that a stolen apple would have created misery—for himself and for his beloved mother. He had nearly ruined everything.

"That is what would have happened, child, with a stolen apple." Aslan's words brought a shiver of excitement. "It is not what will happen now." Digory could not believe his ears! The Lion was giving him an apple to bring home to his mother. When eaten at the right time, in the right way, the apple would heal rather than poison; cure rather than kill; bring joy rather than misery, good instead of bad. Unlike the Witch, Digory would get what he wanted and he *would* like it!

* * * * *

A command was given. A lie was spun and embraced. And to this day, we are living with the terrible fallout.

Then the serpent said to the woman, "You will not surely die. For God knows that in the day you eat of it your eyes will be opened, and you will be like God, knowing good and evil." (GENESIS 3:4-5)

Adam and Eve were warned about the fruit of the tree in the middle of the garden. It was their only restriction, a symbol of their freedom to accept or reject God's offer of intimacy. The tree was placed in the garden not to tempt but to testify. It stood as a daily reminder to Adam and Eve that they could enjoy God's loving protection or chart their own course. The choice was made clear. The consequences were explained. But the deception was sweet and the enticement great.

So when the woman saw that the tree was good for food, that it was pleasant to the eyes, and a tree desirable to make one wise, she took of its fruit and ate. She also gave to her husband with her, and he ate.

(GENESIS 3:6)

Shaken by a lie and driven by desire, the human race chose to follow the lead of our own White Witch—a serpentine liar named Lucifer. At that fateful moment, knowledge beyond purity entered our existence. We quickly discovered that life apart from God is a cold, dark, barren place. And there is no turning back. The dark juice of the apple stains our face as its misery invades our lives. We got what we wanted. But we do not like it.

There is a way that seems right to a man, but its end is the way of death. (PROVERBS 14:12)

God is many things: love, justice, beauty, holiness, wisdom, light, joy. In short, goodness. The opposite of these things—hate, injustice, ugliness, evil, folly, darkness, misery—is the essence of what God is not. When we refuse to submit our lives to the good that He is, we automatically embrace the bad. We can either face the light of the sun, or turn around and see the shadow our choice has cast. Either way, the decision is ours to make. God will not force Himself onto anyone. He is a lover, not a rapist.

In *The Great Divorce*, C. S. Lewis wrote that there are only two kinds of people in the end: those who say to God "Thy will be done," and those to whom God says, in the end, "Thy will be done."[10] Digory chose to submit himself to Aslan's will, resisting the temptation to chart his own course. As a result, he avoided the misery and death that are part of who God isn't and received the joy and life that are part of who He is.

I have set before you life and death, blessing and cursing; therefore choose life, that both you and your descendants may live; that you may love the Lord your God, that you may . . . cling to Him, for He is your life and the length of your days. (DEUTERONOMY 30:19-20)

REFLECTION
When we reject the good God is,
we embrace the evil He isn't.

"But do you really mean, Sir,"
said Peter, "that there could be
other worlds—all over the place,
just round the corner—like that?"

—*THE LION, THE WITCH AND THE WARDROBE*,
CHAPTER 5, "BACK ON THIS SIDE OF THE
DOOR"

CHINKS AND CHASMS

*

Lucy sat sipping her tea and gazing at the portrait of a gray-bearded Faun that hung above the mantelpiece. A fire burned bright upon the hearth; a few wisps of white steam trailed up toward the ceiling from the kettle on the hob. She sighed, a happy, incredulous sigh. She felt exactly as one might feel upon coming home after a long journey.

Setting the cup down, she cast her eyes around the little cave. Slowly, luxuriously she took it all in: the rustic dresser, the oak sideboard lined with blue-patterned china, the reddish stone walls, the carpet and the braided rugs. Near at hand stood a shelf filled with an enticing assortment of books. In particular Lucy noted two volumes bound in dusky red: *Men, Monks and Gamekeepers; a Study in Popular Legend* and *Is Man a Myth?*

"Aren't you hungry, Daughter of Eve?" asked her companion, a curly-haired, curly-horned, goat-footed Faun—a much younger Faun than the one in the painting. He looped his tail up over his arm and stood to pour her another cup. "Wouldn't you like another raspberry tart? Or have my tales of dryads and nymphs begun to bore you?"

Lucy shook herself. "Oh, no, Mr. Tumnus!" she smiled. "It's just that it's all so . . . so *lovely!* And to think that just an hour ago I . . ."

Her voice trailed off and her mind drifted back. Back to England and the war, to blackouts and air raids and raindrops on dirty second-story windows. Back to her brothers and her sister and their morning exploration of the Professor's old manor house. Back to the empty spare room . . . and the wardrobe.

Lucy had known it would be silly to shut herself into a wardrobe. That's why she left the door open when she crept inside . . . just to see what she might see.

At first she saw nothing but mothballs and coats, hooks and wooden rungs. *It's big enough to make an excellent hiding place,* she thought, crawling into the dimness and stretching out her arms toward the wardrobe's back wall.

But there was no wall. *Why, it's even bigger than I thought!* she said to herself. *And so cold!* Something fragrant and prickly brushed her cheek. *Pine boughs?* she wondered. *But how?*

Getting to her feet, she pushed the branches aside. Snow crunched under her shoes. She was standing in a wood, and from a distance a warm, yellowish light was gleaming through the veil of falling snowflakes. There amongst the trees, beneath the glow of an iron lamppost, stood the oddest person she had ever seen: a Faun with an umbrella over his head and a cluster of brown packages under his arm.

Lucy looked up at her host and smiled again. *If it's a dream,* she thought, raising the cup to her lips, *it's been the most perfectly delicious dream I've ever had in my life! I went into a wardrobe and came out here. Will anyone ever believe it?*

* * * * *

From *Star Trek* to *The X-FILES*, from *Harry Potter* to *Buffy the Vampire Slayer*, contemporary fantasy and science fiction are filled with references to the possible existence of parallel dimensions and alternate universes. Everyone, it seems, is fascinated with the idea of other worlds—and the corridors, passageways, or "wormholes" that are supposed to connect them.

C. S. Lewis, creator of *The Chronicles of Narnia*, shared this fascination. He had a term of his own for the "wormholes": chinks and chasms. "There were many chinks or chasms between worlds in old times," said Aslan the great Lion, "but they have grown rarer."[11]

21

Rarer, perhaps, but certainly not excessively rare. For tunnels and passages leading from world to world are the hallmarks of the Narnia stories. Narnia lovers know these "wormholes" well: the Wood between the Worlds; the picture in Aunt Alberta's back bedroom; the door in the wall behind Experiment House.

Lucy stumbled into one of these "chasms." It was the last thing she expected when she crawled into the old wardrobe in the spare room. But that wardrobe, like so many of the corners and cubbyholes in Lewis's imagination, turned out to be bigger on the inside than on the outside. Contrary to all outward appearance, it concealed within its shadowy and camphor-scented depths a cosmic "chink," an unsuspected door into a land of unforeseen wonders.

"I loved the idea of there being doors," says literary critic Francis Spufford, speaking of his earliest introduction to *The Lion, the Witch and the Wardrobe*. "I loved the way there were hidden doors that you could find in unlikely places, like the back of the wardrobe, which would show you that this world *wasn't* all there was; that parts of its walls were actually hinged panels, and they would open, and there was something beyond."[12]

Most of us would agree. It's a tantalizing thought, this notion of a universe where doorways hang in the air and casements open suddenly upon cold, clear distances beyond the stars; where traps and transoms swallow you up and send you tumbling headlong into regions past all human thought or imagination. It's tantalizing because we, like Spufford, have a deep-seated, often inarticulate longing to know that there is, in fact, "something beyond."

If there's a lesson for us in Lucy's adventure with the wardrobe, it's this: Surprise encounters with the unseen world are lurking just around every corner. Divine serendipities lie in ambush at every turn. At any moment we, too, may slip through an undetected crack and find ourselves standing in the middle of a strange and marvelous land, a place beyond the walls of the known universe.

For there *is* such a place. Happily, this workaday world *isn't* all there is. Nearby, just at our elbow, hovering over our heads and brushing past our shoulders, is that "other dimension," where God and the hosts of heaven dwell in power and bliss and unapproachable light. For all its invisibility, it is dangerously real and alarmingly present. And it is ready to burst in upon us, to suck us out of our mundane existence and into a realm of blazing mysteries, just when we least expect it.

This is the good news that Jesus came preaching at the beginning of his Galilean ministry. This, according to the evangelist Mark, was the very first word to fall from His lips when He stepped out onto the stage of His public life: "The time is fulfilled, and the kingdom of God is at hand. Repent, and believe in the gospel" (Mark 1:15).

The kingdom of God is at hand. Not merely "at hand" as in "soon to come," but close, imminent, impending—as near to you as your next heartbeat. As Lucy discovered, another world waits for us just beyond the veil. If only we, like the prophet Elisha's servant (2 Kings 6:17), might be granted eyes to see it! If only we could realize, as poet Francis Thompson has written, that

> *The drift of pinions, would we hearken,*
> *Beats at our own clay-shuttered doors.* [13]

By the grace of God, this gift of "second sight" might descend upon us at any moment. When that moment arrives, we, like Lucy, may find ourselves falling through a cosmic chink and standing face-to-face with an unsuspected Friend, a Friend who meets us at the foot of a tree we didn't know was there, a Friend who calls to us even now through the chinks and chasms of the world:

"I am the door. If anyone enters by Me, he will be saved." (JOHN 10:9)

REFLECTION
The Kingdom of God is nearer than you think.

TURKISH DELIGHT

✳

Edmund was growing bolder by the minute. Braver, more confident, more self-assured. Ever since he'd stepped up into the sledge, his feelings about the mysterious lady in white had begun to change. *She's really not such a bad sort after all,* he told himself. *Besides, she's a queen—didn't she say so herself?*

At first he had hardly dared to speak to her, tall and stern as she was, wrapped all in white fur and crowned with glittering gold. High and lofty she sat on her velvet cushion in the middle of her silver-white sleigh, her face as white as paper, her lips red as rubies, her eyes a piercing blue. What boy wouldn't have been struck dumb at the sight of such a daunting figure?

But now that he was snug beside her, comfortable and

warm beneath the fringe of her soft, expansive robe, everything seemed different. So when she asked him what he'd like to eat, he didn't hesitate for an instant.

"Turkish Delight, please, your Majesty," he said.

And immediately it had appeared in front of him on the snow. Several pounds of the stuff, more than he'd ever seen at one time in his entire life, all wrapped up in a box with a green silk ribbon. Greedily he had wolfed it down, piece after piece, hardly stopping to chew. Never had it tasted so sweet and light, so meltingly delicious to the center of every piece! Edmund barely heard the honeyed words she cooed at him all the while.

By the time the box was empty he'd told her all about his brother and his sisters, the wardrobe, the lamppost, and Lucy's afternoon tea with the Faun. He then promised to bring the others to see her and even accepted an offer to become her adopted son. But the truth was that Edmund wasn't fully aware of what he'd been saying. Even if he *had* known, he wouldn't have cared. All of his thoughts were trained upon a single object: the empty box with the loose green ribbons.

"You *will* bring the others with you?" she said as her sledge pulled away amid the jangle of silver bells. "Because if you *don't* . . ."

"Anything, your Majesty," he answered, feeling a bit dizzy. "If only I might have some more Turkish Delight!"

"Next time!" she called back sweetly through the trees. "Next time! Come soon!" Then she was gone.

"Edmund!"

He turned at the sound of a familiar voice. Someone was approaching from another part of the wood. "*Edmund!* So you've got in too!" It was Lucy!

He smiled weakly. He put out a hand and steadied himself against a tree.

Then, turning away for a moment, he held his stomach and groaned.

* * * * *

A pair of reformed drug addicts were fielding questions from a group of high school students and their parents and teachers.

"Why did you start experimenting with drugs in the first place?" asked one of the kids. "Why did you keep it up? What made you want to move on to the harder stuff?"

The two men exchanged knowing glances; then, as if by mutual consent, one of them stepped up to the microphone and took a deep breath. "You really want to know?" he asked. "It was *fun*."

The reaction from the adults in the room was swift and merciless. "What do you mean?" they protested. "Are you trying to put ideas into these kids' heads?" The meeting soon came to an abrupt and less-than-amiable end.

"Remind me never to ask *them* back again," muttered a disgruntled administrator to a disgusted teacher as they left the room together.

But it was a fair answer. An honest answer. More important, it was an answer that contained a vital element of truth. For drugs couldn't have become the huge and formidable problem they are today unless large numbers of people believed there is some fun to be had from them. And there *is*—at least for a while.

"Stolen water is sweet," observed the Hebrew sage, "and bread eaten in secret is pleasant" (Proverbs 9:17). There *is* something undeniably delectable about illicit pleasures. Untold thrills lurk in the half-concealed gleam of forbidden fruit. If you doubt this, just pluck and taste it. Run to some hidden corner and slowly suck out the juice. You'll have to admit that it's delicious fun—"sweet and light to the very center"—like the Witch's Turkish Delight.

Turkish Delight. It was with a box of this rich and highly addictive British confection that the White Witch first contrived to draw Edmund into the coils of her deadly influence. A big, round box of *enchanted* Turkish Delight, the kind that makes you "want more and more of it." Before he knew what was happening, Edmund had consumed the entire box and was desperate for more.

"Being an American myself," said C. S. Lewis scholar Walter Hooper, "I know that American readers are at a disadvantage when they first encounter the Narnia stories. They're at a disadvantage because *they've never tasted Turkish Delight.* When they *do* taste it, they understand the temptation of Edmund in a new way. For Turkish Delight is irresistible. It's so good that you feel like you'd give your life to go on eating it."[14]

Unfortunately, there's a serious downside to the Epicurean raptures of Turkish Delight. Eat too much of it and your stomach begins to turn. Like the "fun" of drugs or the sweetness of stolen water, like the thrill of an illicit love affair, its savor eventually sours. "Turkish Delight," said Hooper, "soon fails you; very soon it makes you sick."[15]

"Stolen water is sweet,
And bread eaten in secret is pleasant."
But he does not know that the dead are there,
That her guests are in the depths of hell. (PROVERBS 9:17-18)

Edmund was in the process of finding this out for himself when Lucy discovered him in the wood. Already he was feeling "uncomfortable from having eaten too many sweets"; she could see quite clearly that he was a little green around the gills. Did that prevent him from going to unthinkable lengths to procure *another* box of Turkish Delight? No. For in tasting of her treats, Edmund had unwittingly placed himself under the Queen's control. Like Odysseus in the palace of Circe, he had partaken of the enchantress's fare and entered into a binding relationship with her. He had, in effect, sold his soul. That's when his sickness became the sickness unto death.

Some of us understand his position. We've known it from the inside out. Like Edmund, like the confirmed alcoholic, like the husband trapped in a clandestine affair, we've tasted the sweetness of sin and we've come back for more, again and again. We've come back because we've reached a place where there is no other choice; a place of bondage which is not easily broken.

Is it any wonder that the author of Hebrews speaks in such unforgettable terms of "the passing pleasures of sin" (Hebrews 11:25)? Those pleasures do not simply pass *away*. Instead, they pass *into* something entirely unexpected: sorrow and sickness, oppression and involuntary servitude. Ask the former drug addict. There's a reason he's volunteering his time to help high school kids stay clean.

Bread gained by deceit is sweet to a man,
But afterward his mouth will be filled with gravel. (PROVERBS 20:17)

Look—do you see it? Something lying on the snow at your feet. A box: a lovely white box, wrapped like a present and tied with a shiny green bow. Don't ask what's inside; you already know. How could you *not* know when you, like Edmund, placed the order yourself? Now the only question is, will you pick it up? Will you lift the lid? Not in order to know, *but in order to taste?*

Only you can answer.

But before you do, take a moment to remember Edmund.

REFLECTION

Sin's sweetness lasts but a season.

> *People who have not been in Narnia*
> *sometimes think that a thing cannot be*
> *good and terrible at the same time. If*
> *the children had ever thought so, they*
> *were cured of it now.*
>
> —*THE LION, THE WITCH AND THE WARDROBE,*
> CHAPTER 12, "PETER'S FIRST BATTLE"

NOT SAFE BUT GOOD

✳

Peter was panting and blowing as hard as the others by the time they emerged from the shadow of the trees and stepped into the green open space at the top of the hill. He stopped, gulped the air, and cast his eyes around on the scene that lay spread out before them.

On three sides, the dark green forest stretched away downhill into hazy purple distances. Straight ahead and far off to the east something sparkled and danced on the sunlit horizon: the sea. In the center of the grassy hilltop stood an object of dreadful appearance: a great slab of gray stone, supported by four upright stone pillars and engraved all over with swirls and whorls and strange, angular lines. The Stone Table.

Off to one side of the clearing a tall yellow silken pavilion flashed in the sunlight. High into the clear blue air it raised its fluttering pennon, a banner bearing the device of a rampant red lion. In front of the pavilion Peter saw the most peculiar assembly of creatures he had ever laid eyes on——fauns and nymphs and centaurs and Talking Beasts. And in the middle of that crowd, radiant as the sun, silent and terrible as the Stone Table itself, sat the most remarkable figure of all, a huge, dark-maned, honey-colored lion. Peter recognized him at once: *Aslan*——King of the wood, son of the great Emperor-Over-Sea.

"Go on," whispered Mr. Beaver, nudging him. "He's waiting!"

But Peter was trembling like a leaf in the wind. He was remembering what the Beavers had said in answer to their questions about Aslan: "Safe? Who said anything about safe? 'Course he isn't safe. But he's good."

Susan was tugging at his sleeve. "Go ahead," she hissed. "You're the eldest!"

Peter bit his lip and swallowed hard. He drew his sword and raised it to the salute. "Come on," he said to the others. Slowly they advanced.

There was a light in the great beast's eyes like the light of a flame. Peter saw him lift his massy head and gaze upon them as they approached, shaking sparks of sunlight from the heavy curls of his mane.

"Welcome, Peter, Son of Adam," said the lion at last in a deep, rich, and reassuring voice. "Welcome, Susan and Lucy, Daughters of Eve."

The knot in Peter's stomach relaxed. He looked at his sisters and smiled. *It's going to be all right,* he told himself.

* * * * *

God as an alluring but terrifying Question Mark—that's the theme of Rudolf Otto's classic work on man's innate spiritual impulses and religious inclinations, *The Idea of the Holy.* In this book, Otto expounds at length upon his groundbreaking concept of the *mysterium tremendum et fascinans:* the dreadful and attractive mystery of the "Wholly Other."[16]

The apostle Paul might have been thinking of something like this when he assured the pagan Athenians that they had been unwittingly worshiping the true Creator (Acts 17:23). He may have had the same idea in mind when he wrote that sinners are without excuse inasmuch as they already *know God* (Romans 1:21). Everyone is capable of "knowing" Him in this sense. It's simply a matter of paying attention to that quavering little voice at the back of your mind: the whisper that insists there *is* Something Else, something greater and far more powerful than the human mind can comprehend.

The difficulty is that this Something wraps Itself in a cloud of awful uncertainty. Is It friendly? Is It safe? Does It intend to help? How does one go about keeping on Its good side?

Doubts like these have provided the driving force behind pagan religious rite and ritual from the dawn of human history.

Of course, this fear and fascination aren't associated exclusively with primitive or pagan spirituality. We find them in the Bible as well. Job's friend Eliphaz described his own encounter with the *mysterium tremendum et fascinans* in unforgettable language:

In disquieting thoughts from the visions of the night . . .
Fear came upon me, and trembling,
Which made all my bones shake. . . .
Then I heard a voice saying:
"Can a mortal be more righteous than God?
Can a man be more pure than his Maker?" (JOB 4:13-17)

Eliphaz's fears resurfaced with even sharper definition in the experience of the ancient Israelites. They were well acquainted with the terrifying "otherness" of Yahweh. Unlike the Athenian worshipers of the "Unknown God," Moses and his people heard the words of the Lord with their own ears. They saw His mighty works up close. They knew the terror of His presence firsthand:

Now all the people witnessed the thunderings, the lightning flashes, the sound of the trumpet, and the mountain smoking; and when the people saw it, they trembled and stood afar off. Then they said to Moses, "You speak with us, and we will hear; but let not God speak with us, lest we die." (EXODUS 20:18-19)

Even the disciples of Jesus were gripped by a kind of horror when they began to realize who their Master really was:

And they feared exceedingly, and said to one another, "Who can this be, that even the wind and the sea obey Him!" (MARK 4:41)

Trembling, terror, and exceeding fear—Peter Pevensie felt all of this as he stepped out into the open space on the top of the hill of the Stone Table. At his first sight of the great Lion Aslan, he was struck dumb with dread. An awareness that he stood in the presence of incalculable might gripped and held him frozen.

It was a moment of truth. There on that hill Peter realized that power and majesty are fearsome things. He understood that a lion, and *this* Lion in particular, was not something to be toyed with. He conceded the justice of Mr. Beaver's words: "'Course he isn't safe . . .'"

Fortunately, that was not the end of the story. Peter was not left to suffocate beneath a cloud of stifling doubt. Instead, at a nod from Aslan, he gathered his courage and approached the great King. And in so doing he made another discovery, more startling and far more important than the first. He encountered the truth of the second part of Mr. Beaver's assertion: "'Course he isn't safe. But he's good.'"

It was perhaps the most crucial of the many lessons Peter would learn during his sojourn in the land of Narnia. And he learned it in the only way anyone can: He got the message straight from the Lion's mouth. It was as Aslan *spoke* that the boy's fear melted. At his words, uncertainty dispersed like a mist that scatters before the rising sun.

In this scene Lewis gives us a powerful image of the glory of the Christian gospel. Peter's first encounter with Aslan reminds us that there is a divine secret even deeper and more wonderful than Otto's *mysterium tremendum.* God is not merely a terrible and fascinating Question Mark. Instead, He is a Person—a companion, a mentor, a loving protector, and a friend. How do we know this? He told us so Himself.

Come to Me, all you who labor and are heavy laden, and I will give you rest. Take My yoke upon you and learn from Me, for I am gentle and lowly in heart, and you will find rest for your souls.

(MATTHEW 11:28-29)

Not safe but good. That's the kind of lion Peter met on the Hill of the Stone Table. And that's the sort of God we encounter at the hill of Calvary. He's the Rider of Storms and the Lord of Battles. He's the awe-inspiring Architect of the universe. And it just so happens that He "likes well of us."[17]

REFLECTION

We have nothing to fear but the God of grace and love.

FATHER
CHRISTMAS

❄

"It's all right!" Mr. Beaver was shouting from somewhere beyond the mouth of the cave. "Come out, Mrs. Beaver. Come
out, Sons and Daughters of Adam and Eve. It's all right! It
isn't *her!*"

Not her! Lucy hardly dared to believe it. All night long, while
the silent snow drifted down through the arms of the great
trees, she had shivered in the darkness of the underground
burrow, listening breathlessly for the sound of the Witch's
sleigh bells. Through the black hours their dreaded jangle had
haunted her dreams. More than once she had awakened in a
cold sweat, imagining that the Queen was upon them at last.

Then came a moment of truth. In the gray dawn, just

outside the door, the unmistakable ring of harness bells! It was with trembling lip that Lucy had watched Mr. Beaver slip out into the half darkness for a closer look. And now she could hear him calling, "Come out! It isn't *her!*"

Who, then? That's the question that filled every mind as they trudged through the wood toward the clearing. They had their answer as soon as they saw him: a great, glad giant of a man, all in red, with a snowy white beard streaming down over the breast of his ample robe.

"I've got in at last!" boomed Father Christmas, for of course it was he. "She has kept me out for a long time, but her magic is weakening."

Lucy shivered, more with excitement than with the cold. "Always winter and never Christmas"; that's what Mr. Tumnus had said about the Witch's enchantment. "Always winter and never Christmas"; that's the story the Beavers had told them at dinner. It was a dreary, depressing thought. But now, it seemed, all that was about to change. For here *he* was! And "Aslan," she heard Father Christmas saying, "is on the move."

He had gifts for each of them, of course: a sword and a shield for Peter; a bow, quiver, and a little ivory horn for Susan. For Lucy there was a dagger and a wonderful diamond flask filled with a healing cordial. Even the Beavers got presents: a new sewing machine for Mrs. Beaver, and for Mr. Beaver the promise of a finished and mended dam.

"And now," said Father Christmas, smiling, "here is

something for the moment!" And suddenly in the middle of the snowy wood there appeared cups and saucers, cream and sugar, and a great big steaming pot of hot tea.

The best tea I've ever had, thought Lucy as she sat in the cold shadows of the Beaver-burrow, cradling her cup in her hands. Somewhere outside in the growing light, a great voice trumpeted a triumphant farewell: "A Merry Christmas! Long live the true King!"

*   *   *   *   *

Jesus was born in Bethlehem of Judea in the days of Herod the king.

(MATTHEW 2:1)

This brief passage from the Gospel of Matthew contains the very essence of the Christmas message, a message that may come home to us all the more tellingly if we simply reverse the clauses: "In the days of Herod the king, *then* Jesus was born."

They were dark days, bleak days—days devoid of hope for justice-loving, God-fearing, Torah-believing Jews. Herod the Great, ruler of the province of Judea from 37 B.C. to 4 B.C., was without doubt one of the most ruthless and tyrannical princes ever to hold sway over that bloodstained and sorrow-stricken little corner of the world. Herod, master of cruelty and intrigue. Herod, king of envy and paranoia. Herod, a man who could slaughter infants and murder his own wife and sons without batting an eye. *He* was in control when God entered history as a tender, helpless babe, a trembling point of light on the edge of a vast, encircling darkness.

Imagine what it would have been like if that light had never dawned—if that bleakness had gone on without interruption, without variation, without end, like a stone-hard, barren-faced desert stretching to the horizon and down the other side of the world. Christina Rosetti captures the mood in her famous Christmas poem (turned carol) "Mid-Winter":

> *In the bleak mid-winter*
> *Frosty wind made moan,*
> *Earth stood hard as iron,*
> *Water like a stone.*[18]

Unbroken winter, grim and cheerless—such is the backdrop against which the story of *The Lion, the Witch and the Wardrobe* unfolds. No sooner have we stepped into Narnia than we discover that the entire land lies under a shadow every bit as thick and gloomy as the one that covered Judea in the days of Herod the king. For here in Narnia, thanks to the White Witch, it is "always winter and never Christmas."

The imagery hits home with the child in each and every one of us. Just ask any kid. Like a week without a weekend or a school year without the holidays, winter without Christmas would be simply unendurable.

That's why the Celtic and Teutonic tribes of northern Europe invented Yuletide in the first place; at the darkest hour of

the year, they celebrated the return of the light. That's why the flap over the pagan origins of Christmas and the endless debates about the precise timing of Jesus' birth are largely beside the point: They fail to recognize the *symbolic* significance of the Christian appropriation of solstice festivals.

But the symbolism is too beautiful and too powerful to miss. It underscores an aspect of the Christmas message that we dare not neglect. It was *during the days of Herod the king* that the Savior was born. And it is in the "bleak midwinter" of personal failure, heartbreak, and disappointment that Jesus delights to encounter us today. Just as the legendary Christmas rose blooms in the frosts of December, so Christ descends to us in times of emptiness, hopelessness, and barrenness of soul.

It's in such a context that Father Christmas comes sledging onto the stage of the Narnian drama. He makes his entrance to the accompaniment of bells, laughing aloud in the silent, snowy wood. Like Gandalf the White at the edge of Fangorn Forest,[19] he appears at the turn of the tide. Like John the Baptist on the banks of the Jordan, he arises in the desert as a harbinger of hope, a voice crying in the wilderness.

More to the point, Father Christmas comes bearing gifts— gifts that equip; gifts that enable; warming, cheering, heartening gifts. All these and more come tumbling out of the bulging sack atop his sleigh. And when the presents have all been handed out, he does an even more remarkable thing. In the cold, unnatural stillness of the bewitched world, he produces a cozy reminder of homely hospitality: a steaming pot of tea. It's more than just a bit of momentary comfort. It's a promise. For as the tea is poured and the sugar passed, Narnia is shaken to its foundations with the expectation of coming change.

For lo, the winter is past,
The rain is over and gone.
The flowers appear on the earth;
The time of singing has come. (SONG OF SOLOMON 2:11-12)

Are you listening? Did you hear? It isn't her—it's *Him.* The witch's magic is weakening! You thought it would last forever, but the ice is melting and the winter of your discontent is drawing to an end. This is the meaning of Father Christmas's unforeseen appearance in the Narnian woods. It's also the intensely real, eternally rock-solid, and deeply personal significance of the birth of Jesus—that same Jesus who was born *during the days of Herod the king.* Therefore, take heart, "for now our salvation is nearer than when we first believed" (Romans 13:11).

"Do not, I beseech you, be troubled about the increase of forces already in dissolution. You have mistaken the hour of the night. It is already morning."[20]

REFLECTION
God is the God of new beginnings.

> *"When a willing victim who had committed no treachery was killed in a traitor's stead, the Table would crack and Death itself would start working backwards."*
>
> —*THE LION, THE WITCH AND THE WARDROBE,* CHAPTER 15, "DEEPER MAGIC FROM *BEFORE* THE DAWN OF TIME"

DEEP AND DEEPER MAGIC

✳

It was so cold! Lucy beat her arms against her body and stamped her feet. Aching with weariness, dazed and dizzy, she took a few stumbling steps away from the Stone Table and looked out to the east. A single bright star blazed above the pale horizon.

Horrible images from the previous night washed over her like a black tide. The blood red torches. The leering faces of the Hags, Ogres, and Wraiths. The ropes and the muzzle. The shearing of poor Aslan's mane. Again she saw the moonlight burning cold along the stone knife's whetted edge. Again she shuddered at the Witch's triumphant shriek and heard her

cruel taunts: "Fool! Now I will kill you instead of the human traitor and so the Deep Magic will be appeased!"

"Lucy—" Susan's voice interrupted her thoughts—"let's walk about a bit. Just to keep warm."

"Yes, let's," agreed Lucy.

Back and forth, then, between the dead Aslan and the brow of the hill, the girls paced while the sky grew light overhead. Neither of them had a single tear left to shed; all had been spent during the long dark hours of the dreadful night. Except for the first stirrings of birdsong among the trees, silence reigned within and all around them.

They paused a moment to watch as the rim of the sun emerged from the eastern sea like a bubble of molten gold. Lucy felt utterly blank and empty inside. It was as if the whole world had come to an end. She groped for Susan's hand.

Crack!

From behind them came a deafening noise like the shattering of the sky itself. The girls jumped. Lucy glanced at her sister's pale face. Then they turned and ran.

At the top of the hill they stopped and stared. The Stone Table lay on the ground in two broken fragments. The body of Aslan was gone.

"What *now?*" wailed Lucy. "Haven't they done enough already?"

But Susan put a hand upon her shoulder. "Wait," she said. "Do you think it could be more magic?"

"Yes!" cried a voice like morning thunder. "It *is* more magic!"

They wheeled around. "Aslan!" they shouted—for it was the Lion himself, bright as the sun and larger than they remembered him. "Dear Aslan! Aren't you dead?"

"Not anymore!" he answered. "This is a Magic the Witch knew nothing about. A Deeper Magic! The Magic of a blameless victim who willingly lays down his life for another. And now, dear children," he added, shaking his golden mane and bounding across the hilltop, "death has begun to work backwards. I feel life throbbing and pulsing within me again. Come! Let us run and play!"

And together they romped and tumbled in the morning light.

* * * * *

Good fantasy writers know that consistency is the key to believable "sub-creation."[21] Invented worlds are convincing (and thus truly enchanting) precisely to the extent that they remain faithful to their own foundational principles. If a storyteller informs us that a sleeping princess can be awakened only by true love's first kiss, then she must sleep on, for a hundred years if necessary, until Prince Charming arrives. If rings of power can be unmade only in the fires that forged them, then we cannot hope to destroy them in any other way. Rules, once established, must be rigorously observed; otherwise the house of cards falls to the ground.

It's in this strictness and symmetry of design that fantasy

provides us with one of its most instructive mirror images of the real world. God's universe, too, is founded upon inviolable precepts and ordinances. The stars and planets keep their ancient courses. Summer and winter, springtime and harvest follow one another in invariable sequence. The Lord has "laid the foundations of the earth"—physical, moral, and spiritual—"so that it should not be moved forever" (Psalm 104:5).

This law of fixed and constant principles is precisely what Lewis had in mind when he wrote about the "magic" of Narnia. For Narnian magic, at its heart, has nothing to do with spells or potions or incantations. Narnian magic, by contrast, is a question of primal patterns, of unbreakable connections and necessary relationships. It's a matter of knowing the rules and playing by them.

There was a Deep Magic at work in the land of Narnia, an unshakable natural law, firm as the roots of the mountains themselves. According to this magic, any act of treason leads inevitably to death. Anyone who overthrows or subverts absolute allegiance to the Emperor-Over-Sea and his son automatically forfeits his life. Moreover, every traitor's blood belongs to the Witch—as she knows all too well.

A similar magic has been built into our own world. God warned Adam and Eve about it in the Garden of Eden:

"But of the tree of the knowledge of good and evil you shall not eat, for in the day that you eat of it you shall surely die." (GENESIS 2:17)

The principle is reaffirmed in the words of the prophets—"the soul who sins shall die" (Ezekiel 18:4; see also Jeremiah 31:30)—and in the writings of the apostle Paul— "the wages of sin is death" (Romans 6:23). The connection this principle draws between sin and death is not merely an expression of divine vengeance or punishment. On the contrary, it is inherent to the very fabric of creation. It grows directly out of the unfailing consistency of God's own character. It's a corollary of the unalterable righteousness by which He declares, "I, the Lord your God, am a jealous God, visiting the iniquity of the fathers upon the children to the third and fourth generations of those who hate Me" (Exodus 20:5). As in Lewis's invented world, this deep magic *must* be appeased. To ignore its demands is to invite the dissolution of the cosmos itself.

But there is another magic bubbling at the core of the Narnian universe. It erupts in a burst of unexpected glory when Susan and Lucy hear the loud *crack!* of the Stone Table's sudden collapse. The girls feel its earthshaking energy when, at the sound of a mighty shout, they turn to see the great Lion Aslan—he who was slain in the traitor's stead—restored to life and laughing in the sunrise.

In that moment the Witch's victory is overturned. The Deep Magic is trumped by an even deeper power. The rule of forfeiture and fair returns is swallowed up in the prior principle of grace, mercy, and atonement. And death itself, as Aslan triumphantly declares, begins to work backward.

The same holds true in the real world. For *The Lion, the Witch and the Wardrobe*'s astounding climax is really just a fictional reminder of the most fundamental of all Christian truths. Christ, like Aslan, has died and risen again on our behalf. By His sacrifice, He has broken the spell of sin and death. But that's not all. What is every bit as important, but far less obvious, is the fact that His atoning death was neither an afterthought nor a hastily adopted provisional measure—a kind of plan B thrown together at the last minute as a way of dealing with unforeseen complications. On the contrary, it flows out of the oldest and most profound of all the Creator's designs and plans: God's original, primeval intention to lay down His life for His friends.

This is why John refers to Christ as "the Lamb slain from the foundation of the world" (Revelation 13:8; see also I Peter 1:20). In the end, the deepest magic of all is the magic of God's redeeming and self-sacrificing love, the love that is in itself the soul of creation, the hub of the wheel, and the fulcrum upon which everything moves and turns.

REFLECTION

The universe is founded on God's redeeming love.

SONS OF ADAM AND DAUGHTERS OF EVE

❋

Never had Edmund felt so profoundly humbled and so strangely exalted all in the same moment. He stood blinking in the colored light of Cair Paravel's high-arched windows. Kaleidoscopic images, like the pictures in the stained glass, tumbled one over the other inside his head: first the Lion and the Witch; then the knife and the Stone Table, battles and wounds, strange faces in feverish dreams. And now—crowns and thrones! A castle and a kingdom! It was enough to make any boy dizzy.

Catching his breath, he turned to gape at the splendor of the Great Hall. At his feet glittered the tessellated reds, greens, and yellows of the tiled mosaic floor. Above his head the carved ribs and rafters of the ivory ceiling reflected the glow of the chandeliers in tints of creamy pink and subtle orange. The west door was radiant with the rainbow hues of peacock feathers. The east door, wide open to the sea, let in the haunting strains of the mermen and mermaids' song. Beside him stood his two sisters and his brother, radiant in blue and scarlet and white. At their throats and on their arms flashed chains and bracelets of lustrous gold. Edmund fingered the sapphire amulet that dangled from his own neck and shook his head in happy disbelief.

Down the middle of the floor, from one end of the hall to the other, stretched a wide runner of rich red velvet. Ranged along either side of this carpet were the beaming faces of the children's Narnian friends: Mr. and Mrs. Beaver, Tumnus the Faun, Giant Rumbebuffin; centaurs and unicorns, Dwarfs and dryads, Talking Beasts of every kind. And he and Peter and Susan and Lucy were to rule over these good creatures as kings and queens! So said the ancient prophecy. He blushed and trembled at the thought.

Suddenly the west door swung open and there stood Aslan, silhouetted hugely in the bright open space. Every head turned, every eye fixed itself upon the Lion's majestic form as he padded slowly down the aisle, an unearthly glow in his eyes. Edmund flinched involuntarily; then, with an effort, he raised his head and let those yellow eyes fix him in their gaze.

With great ceremony, the Lion led them down to the dais at the other end of the room. There he seated them upon four thrones of ivory and gold, put scepters into their hands, and crowned them with circlets of gold. At last he spoke. "Once a king or queen in Narnia, always a king or queen. Bear it well, Sons of Adam! Bear it well, Daughters of Eve!"

The assembly erupted in thunderous cheers and shouts. The rafters shook, the chandeliers shimmered, and the centaurs stamped with their silver-shod hooves.

As for Edmund, he was overwhelmed with the strangest, most unexpected feeling, a feeling of coming home at last.

* * * * *

What does it mean to be human? What is it that sets a man or a woman apart from the beasts of the field, the birds of the air, and the fish of the sea? Why does human nature seem so *unnatural?* Some of our greatest minds have wanted to know.

"The simplest truth about man," wrote G. K. Chesterton, "is that he is a very strange being; almost in the sense of being a stranger on the earth."[22] Chesterton wasn't alone in this observation. Seventeenth century poet Alexander Pope reflected on this strangeness when he described humanity as "the glory, jest, and riddle of the world."[23] Socrates, greatest of the ancient Greek philosophers, felt it from within. "I want to know . . . about myself," he said. "Am I a monster more complicated and swollen with passion than the serpent Typho, or a creature of a gentler and simpler sort?"[24]

Even the Bible *raises* the issue of human identity and significance far more often than it attempts to *resolve* it. "Lord, what is man," cried the psalmist, "that You take knowledge of him?" (Psalm 144:3). And also,

When I consider Your heavens, the work of Your fingers,
The moon and the stars, which You have ordained,
What is man that You are mindful of him,
And the son of man, that You visit him? (PSALM 8:3-4)

In *The Chronicles of Narnia*, C. S. Lewis offers a bold and bracing answer to this question, a response as alarming as it is exhilarating. The perspective on people that unfolds as we penetrate Lewis's imaginary world is both breathtaking and frightening, pregnant with promise and fraught with food for sober reflection. For the deeper we travel into Narnia, the clearer it becomes that the inhabitants of its enchanted woods—fauns and centaurs and Talking Beasts—regard human beings as something altogether extraordinary. With few exceptions, they agree that "Sons of Adam and Daughters of Eve" are *destined to rule.*

Four thrones at Cair Paravel; four thrones shrouded in mystery, antiquity, and shades of ancient prophecy. Only when "two Sons of Adam and two Daughters of Eve" sit upon these thrones will the world be right at last, so says an old rhyme that has been repeated in Narnia since time out of mind. The fate of Aslan's world, it seems, is bound up with the fate of humankind. We are not surprised, then, when the children's adventures in Narnia draw to their inevitable conclusion; in the end, Peter, Susan, Edmund, and Lucy must rise to the throne. In our world, too, men and women are meant to have dominion over the earth. God has designed them, among other purposes, to rule with Him as vice regents of creation. Only humans, of all the creatures formed of clay, have been stamped with the image of their Creator (Genesis 1:27). Only they partake of *His* breath (Genesis 2:7) and bear the imprint of *His* character. Thus, they alone possess the rights and responsibilities of heirs.

For You have made him a little lower than the angels,
And You have crowned him with glory and honor.
You have made him to have dominion over the works of Your hands.

(PSALM 8:5-6)

In *The Weight of Glory,* Lewis reflects powerfully upon the implications of mankind's royal endowment:

> It is a serious thing to live in a society of possible gods and goddesses, to remember that the dullest and most uninteresting person you talk to may one day be a creature which, if you saw it now, you would be strongly tempted to worship, or else a horror and a corruption such as you now meet, if at all, only in a nightmare.[25]

A sobering thought. For we must remember that the horror and corruption would certainly eclipse every other possibility were it not for the redeeming work of the Second Adam (I Corinthians 15:47). Jesus Christ is *the* great Son of Man, the King of kings to whom all crowns and thrones belong. In Him and Him alone can we be fully restored to our rightful place as sub-creators[26] and corulers of God's world:

Assuredly I say to you, that in the regeneration, when the Son of Man sits on the throne of His glory, you who have followed Me will also sit on twelve thrones, judging the twelve tribes of Israel.

(MATTHEW 19:28)

"It is a serious thing to live in a society of possible gods and goddesses." It's even more serious to *be* those "possible gods and goddesses," to accept the challenge of preparing ourselves, by faith and obedience to the King, not only to bear the weight of that eternal glory, but to shoulder the burden of the God-given responsibility it confers.

REFLECTION
Our humanness is a great and terrible responsibility.

IRRESISTIBLY DRAWN

❋

It was a dull, drowsy autumn afternoon. Lucy sat on the hard wooden bench in the little country station, listening to the buzzing of a fly and staring alternately at her shoes, the empty tracks in front of the platform, and the grayish green blur of gorse bushes on the hill beyond the tracks.

Summer gone, she thought, giving her big black traveling case an idle kick. *Holidays over.* There was a lump in her throat and a flutter in the pit of her stomach: Lucy had never been to boarding school before. She sighed and cast a furtive glance down the bench at Peter, Susan, and Edmund. They all looked as if they hadn't a care in the world.

Turning away, she squinted out across the fields. Was

that a hawk wheeling in the distance? Was that a rabbit on the ground, trying to evade the predator's penetrating eye?

"Oh!" Lucy jumped. Someone—or something—had touched her.

"What's wrong, Lu?" said Edmund as she turned to face him. "Anyone would think you'd—*Ow!*" And he, too, jerked violently to one side and gave a startled cry.

"Susan!" shouted Peter at the same instant. "Let go!"

"I'm not touching you!" objected Susan. "But I feel it too—as if some invisible person were *pulling* on me—as if I were being dragged along!"

"Exactly!" agreed Lucy. "And it's getting worse. I can't stand it!"

Edmund was on his feet. "It's magic!" he shouted. "Everyone join hands. We're in for a ride!"

"I believe you're right!" agreed Peter.

Suddenly everything went black. An instant more and the darkness gave way to a swirling eddy of light and shadow. A moment later they all opened their eyes (for of course they had shut them very tightly) and found that the bench, the platform, the railroad tracks, and the hills had all vanished.

"Look!" said Peter. They were standing in a thick wood or coppice. Through the treetops bright yellow sunlight shone down out of a brilliant blue sky. Between the white trunks they could see a smooth, sandy beach and the gentle swell of a tranquil inlet of the sea.

"Narnia!" cried Lucy. "We've been pulled into *Narnia!*"

They looked at one another in amazement. It was true.

And somewhere in Narnia at that very moment, across the crystal bay and the dark green woods beyond, a long, clear, musical note was just fading into silence—the note of a silver horn sounding the cry for help.

* * * * *

Prince Caspian: The Return to Narnia. Such is the title under which the second of the seven Chronicles of Narnia was released in 1951 and by which it has been known to enthusiastic readers ever since. What most of those readers don't realize is that the author wasn't entirely happy with the name. If Lewis had had *his* way, this story would have been called *Drawn into Narnia.*[27]

Thereby hangs a tale, a tale that is something more than just a bit of historical trivia. For Lewis's original title preserves and underscores one of the driving concepts behind the engaging sequel to *The Lion, the Witch and the Wardrobe:* the idea of an adventure undertaken in response to an irresistible summons or call.

We've already suggested that the notion of passageways between parallel worlds is essential not only to the dramatic interest but to the spiritual significance of Lewis's imaginary universe. *Prince Caspian* begins with a striking variation on this theme. In every other case, it's a question of someone seeking, finding, or stumbling upon the door to the otherworld. Here, by contrast, it's a matter of being *dragged* or *pulled* through.

"Jack Lewis wanted the reader to sense immediately the idea of being drawn or pulled into another world," said the author's stepson Douglas Gresham in his introduction to Focus on the Family Radio Theatre's dramatic adaptation of *Prince Caspian:*

> Lewis observed that in many fantasy stories characters were summoned by magic, and that these stories were told from the point of view of the magician, or the one who had done the summoning. He wondered what it would be like to be on the receiving end of the summons, to be suddenly pulled from our world into another world. That was the beginning of the idea for *Prince Caspian.* [28]

Out of that initial idea grew the details of the book's opening scene. Peter, Susan, Edmund, and Lucy sat in an English country station, waiting for a train that would take them to school. Suddenly, without warning, they were supernaturally seized and snatched away—"drawn into Narnia" in response to Caspian's sounding of Queen Susan's magic horn, the horn that was said to bring help to anyone who blew it.

What would it be like to be on the receiving end of such a summons? We all have a personal interest in the answer to that question. As a matter of fact, if we belong to Christ, we already *know* the answer. Everyone who has had an authentic encounter with the living God understands what it means to be snapped up out of the mundane world of everyday existence and hauled willy-nilly into the kingdom of heaven. In one way or another, it's a part of every normal Christian life.

The apostle Paul was certainly familiar with the experience. Allegiance to a crucified carpenter was the last thing he had in mind when he set out on the road to Damascus. His plan was to annihilate the hated sect of the Nazarene. But God had a different idea. And so, in a blinding flash, Paul's goals and orientation changed. He was knocked down and dragged, kicking and screaming as it were, into a whole new world.

There are plenty of other examples, of course. Gideon was attending to business as usual when the angel of the Lord nabbed him and said, "Go. . . . Have I not sent you?" (Judges 6:14). Isaiah's life took a radical turn when a vision gripped him and a voice cried, "Whom shall I send?" (Isaiah 6:8). Peter was snagged in the Great Fisherman's net (Mark 1:16-18). Levi was snatched out of his tax-booth and lured away by the magnetism of the Master (Luke 5:27-28).

The message is plain. We approach God not because we decide to, but because He reaches out and draws us to Himself. We follow Him because He pulls us along. He woos us by the compelling, constraining power of His irresistible grace. We love Him because He first loved us (I John 4:19).

No one can come to Me unless the Father who sent Me draws him; and I will raise him up at the last day. (JOHN 6:44)

I have loved you with an everlasting love; therefore with lovingkindness I have drawn you. (JEREMIAH 31:3)

The life of faith is a pilgrimage that no one should undertake lightly. Indeed, no one *can.* And this, believe it or not, can be a comforting thought. There is tremendous reassurance in the reflection that we enter upon this adventure only because, like the Pevensies, we are specially chosen and called, because we are hooked, caught, and reeled in by the irresistible power of the Savior's love. Out of that foundational truth flows the strength to accept the challenge, the energy to accomplish the mission, and the endurance to reach the journey's end in triumph and joy.

REFLECTION

The greatest adventure is the one that is thrust upon us.

OLD NARNIANS

❄

Caspian was breathless with excitement. Positioning himself
under the branches of a spreading oak, he tightened his
sword belt and surveyed the scene with a sense of deep satisfaction. The much anticipated gathering was coming together before his very eyes. From every direction they were
pouring out of the surrounding forest and into the open expanse of Dancing Lawn: centaurs and Fauns, stags and unicorns, Dwarfs, satyrs, and every kind of Talking Beast. There
was even a small army of Talking Mice and a lumbering,
stumbling Giant. As they stepped out from between the
trees, their sharp, black shadows leaping crazily over the
dewy, moon-silvered grass, Caspian couldn't help but smile

at their wild appearance. Never in his life had he seen such a gloriously motley crew.

Fingering the jeweled pommel of his dwarf-made sword, the young king (yes—these strange people actually called him *king*) lifted his chin and gazed up into the star-spattered Narnian sky. A pleasant glow rose from his heart to his head as he thought back to that first unexpected meeting with Trufflehunter, the wise and solemn badger, and the dwarfs Trumpkin and Nikabrik. It seemed an age ago; in reality, it hadn't been more than a few weeks. Once more he smiled, recalling how he had responded to their offer to send him home: "I don't want to go. I've been looking for people like you all my life."

It was true. From the cradle Caspian had listened to his nurse tell of the Old Narnians—the people who lived out in the wild places, preserving the old tales and holding fast to the old ways. Her stories about Aslan, the Talking Beasts, and the ancient kings and queens of Cair Paravel had been food to his soul and light to his eyes all through those cruel years in the house of King Miraz. For as long as he could remember, the boy had been wishing—wishing so hard that it hurt sometimes—that the people in the stories might somehow turn out to be real. And now, beyond all belief, he had found them. It was like a kind of homecoming.

"Shall I have everyone sit down on the grass, sire?" someone shouted in his ear, for the chatter of the creatures had become a veritable din. "Shouldn't we get this council under way?"

Caspian turned. At his side stood Glenstorm the lordly centaur—prophet, stargazer, seer, and guide. His flowing hair and beard shone red gold in the moonlight, his back and flanks a glossy chestnut brown. Keen and sharp were his piercing blue eyes; his finely chiseled face was both somber and joyous. For a moment the king could only blink and stare. Was this actually happening? Could the vision be real?

"By all means, Glenstorm," he answered, quickly recovering his composure. "It's time we got down to business. Tarva and Alambil have met in the heavens. The long years of waiting are over. The moment has arrived for the people in hiding to arise."

✳   ✳   ✳   ✳   ✳

"Enemy-occupied territory—that is what this world is," said Lewis in *Mere Christianity*.[29] In these few words he sums up a concept that is foundational not only to a biblical understanding of Creation and the fall (see chapter 2, "Evil Has Entered") but also to a working view of the church in the world today.

Think of a military outpost—or more accurately, a network of small, interrelated outposts—operating behind enemy lines. Think of the French Resistance: a loosely organized coalition of farmers, shopkeepers, and pastrymen working underground to subvert the Nazi occupation. Think of the Old Narnians: a strange mix of animals, dwarfs, and mythological creatures, hiding out in the mountains, honoring the memory of Cair Paravel and High King Peter, waiting for the return of Aslan, the great Lion. In its own way, each of these pictures contains a clue to *our* identity as followers of Jesus. Each can help us grasp more clearly the position of the Christian community in the midst of contemporary secular society.

Not that the situation we face is uniquely modern. Far from it. Granted, a great deal has been said and written in recent years about the decline of the West and the threat of postmodernism. Much of this talk is completely accurate and entirely justified. Still, we must be careful not to give the doomsayers more credit than they deserve. If as Christians we look around and find ourselves outnumbered and outgunned, we must remember that there is no special cause for alarm. For the true people of God have *always* been a small and faithful remnant surrounded by a large, unbelieving majority—an odd assortment of renegades, nonconformists, and social outcasts, like the Old Narnians who lived in exile amongst the wooded hills.

Remnant theology is a thread that appears early in the story of God's relations with man and grows thicker, stronger, and more apparent as it weaves its way through the tapestry of the biblical narrative. It begins with Abraham's call, runs through the account of the Exodus, and continues in the history of the wilderness wanderings. It shows up again and again in the chronicles of the divided kingdom, the Exile, and the restoration. It resurfaces dramatically in the Gospels' portrait of Jesus and His tiny following of fishermen, tax collectors, and zealot revolutionaries. It persists in the New Testament's description of the primitive Christian community—"aliens, scattered throughout Pontus, Galatia, Cappadocia, Asia, and Bithynia" (I Peter 1:1, NASB).

"My father was a wandering Aramean," chanted the ancient Israelite, "and he went down to Egypt and sojourned there, few in number" (Deuteronomy 26:5, NASB). David echoed this thought in his confession that God gave the land of Canaan to His people "when [they] were few in number, indeed very few, and strangers in it" (I Chronicles 16:19). David himself spent what may have been the most formative period of his life hiding out in the desert with a small, tight-knit troop of loyal guerrilla fighters. Jesus appeared to be working from a similar set of assumptions when He told His disciples that the way to life is narrow and difficult "and there are few who find it" (Matthew 7:14).

In view of all this, should believers ever be surprised to find themselves in the minority? Hardly. What *if* the atheists and secular humanists gain the upper hand? What *if* the media mock the biblical faith? What *if* prayer is outlawed and Christians marginalized? Would David be shaken? Would Elijah be shocked? Would Jesus be caught off guard? Not likely. On the contrary, they would probably take a look around, shrug their shoulders, and say, "Appears to be 'situation normal.' Now let's get back to work."

"Though your people, O Israel, be as the sand of the sea," wrote Isaiah, "a remnant of them will return" (Isaiah 10:22). *This* is the Bible's most characteristic picture of the assembly of the saved and blessed: not a conquering army terrible with banners, but a few stubborn survivors straggling back to claim their rightful inheritance. *This* is Scripture's most recurrent portrait of the true church: a fellowship of unlikely heroes who overcome their enemy not in strength of numbers or by dint of force, but by the blood of the Lamb, by the word of their testimony, and by not loving their lives unto death (Revelation 12:11). It's Caspian and the Old Narnians all over again.

Would you like to join this hard-pressed but happy band? Have you, like Caspian, been looking for such people all your life? If so, you're in luck. Enrollment is open and newcomers are always welcome. And, as in the case of the people who lived in hiding on the edge of Narnia's western waste, the promise of the long-awaited payback has just appeared on the horizon. The true King is returning; we expect His arrival at any moment. Indeed, as Lewis put it, He has already landed.[30]

In the meantime, our task is to stand firm and keep the faith.

REFLECTION
The true church is an underground resistance movement.

STRANGE HELP

❄

"You've sounded your precious horn," said Nikabrik, his black beard wagging at the end of his chin, "and precious little good has come of it! I say we shift course!"

Caspian winced under the lash of the Dwarf's sharp tongue and stared down at the little ivory horn. Yellow-white, it gleamed in the faint candlelight. He shook his head. How could he have placed so much confidence in such a small thing?

Looking up, he scanned the anxious faces ranged around the rough wooden council table. A small thing, yes; and yet supposedly a thing of great virtue. Doctor Cornelius had told him that the horn of Queen Susan would bring help—strange help—to anyone who blew it. But the horn had been sounded and no help had arrived.

"I must admit," said Doctor Cornelius, speaking slowly and deliberately, "that I am deeply disappointed in the result of the operation. I have always believed the old tales. I fully expected assistance to come. But now—"

"Now you'd better take *my* advice!" interrupted Nikabrik. "Practical power—*that's* what's wanted. That's what my friends here"—he indicated two gaunt, shadowy figures lurking on the edge of the circle of light—"can bring to this table: the kind of power that made it always winter in Narnia and never Christmas for a hundred years!"

"Power—yes!" croaked one of the dark shapes. "The power of the White Witch."

Caspian was on his feet in an instant, sword in hand. "You *dare* speak of the Witch? Even here—at Aslan's How?"

"This is vain, useless blasphemy," said Trufflehunter. "The help *will* come, I assure you. Perhaps even now it waits at the door."

"At the door, you say?" sneered Nikabrik. "Show it to me, then!"

With that the dwarf drew his own blade and leapt atop the table. Caspian made a move to fend off the blow. But in the next moment one of the gray shapes was upon him, burying its teeth in his arm. He screamed in pain and struck out with his right foot, overturning the table, dashing the light, and plunging the chamber into darkness. For the next few minutes all was a confused din of shouts, howls, and clashing steel.

When Caspian came to, he found himself looking up into the face of a boy about his own age. Candlelight flickered over the walls. Nikabrik and his friends lay dead.

"King Caspian?" said the strange boy.

The young king blinked. "Wh-who are you?" he stammered.

"Birdbaths and buttonholes, your Majesty!" came a familiar voice, laughing—the voice of Trumpkin the Dwarf. "Don't you know? It's the High King. King Peter himself! We've been standing outside that door the longest time!"

* * * * *

Anyone who longs for God's kingdom as badly as Caspian wanted to rediscover the Old Narnia is almost certain to run into the predicament he encountered in the dark chamber at the heart of Aslan's How. It's the dilemma of disillusionment and dashed hopes. It's the problem of disappointment with God.

Disappointment is the fruit of failed expectations. It's what happens when your taste buds are primed for cheesecake and you get watery oatmeal instead. The etymology of the word is instructive, for its component elements (from French and Latin) conjure up images of errancy in archery or frustration on the riflery range. Picture yourself at target practice: You draw a bead on the bull's-eye, sight carefully along the barrel, squeeze the trigger, and—someone bumps your shoulder and sends your shot astray. Your aim is thwarted. That's disappointment.

We become disappointed with God when His behavior doesn't fit the paradigms and patterns we've established for Him in our own minds, just as Caspian and Cornelius became disheartened when Queen Susan's horn failed to produce the kind of assistance they were expecting to receive. Not that the horn didn't work; in actuality, it couldn't have been more effective. But the help it brought was *strange*—almost too strange to be recognized.

This strangeness surfaces again and again in the story of *Prince Caspian.* The children run up against it the moment they arrive in Narnia. Who could have guessed that the dilapidated ruin in the midst of the overgrown island would turn out to be Cair Paravel, the grand castle where once they had ruled as kings and queens? Who would have surmised that the Lion would send a group of English schoolchildren to rescue the Old Narnians from King Miraz and his powerful army? Who, indeed, would have supposed that Aslan himself could behave in such an odd, unpredictable manner? "Why should Aslan be invisible to us?" complained Peter at a crucial point in the story. "He never used to be. It's not like him."[31]

The blackest moment, of course, came during Caspian's

eleventh-hour council meeting at Aslan's How. The horn had been blown, apparently without effect. Time appeared to be running out. Under the circumstances, one could hardly blame Nikabrik for proposing an alternate plan, however dark and sinister. But it was precisely at this juncture that the long-awaited help—strange, unexpected help—stepped out of the otherworld and into the darkened chamber in the form of Peter and Edmund Pevensie. As Trufflehunter had so rightly predicted, it was waiting at the door all the time.

It's not like Him. Have you ever felt that way about God? If so, you're not alone. A moment's reflection—and some serious scriptural study—should be enough to persuade us that God usually works in unusual ways. He's the Lord of the roller coaster, the Master Engineer of the winding cliffside road. He delights in unforeseen twists and turns. When we become locked into our own preconceived notions and plans, we run the risk of missing out on the adventure of *His* choosing. But if we're willing to let go of our personal goals and visions—and to suffer the pain, the heartache, and the disillusionment this often entails—we can look forward to the ride of our lives. The turnaround always comes when the prospects look bleakest. In the words of novelist Fyodor Dostoevsky:

> But I predict that just when you see with horror that in spite of all your efforts you are getting farther from

your goal instead of nearer to it—at that very moment I predict that you will reach it and behold clearly the miraculous power of the Lord who has been all the time loving and mysteriously guiding you.[32]

Disappointment with God. Mary and Martha experienced it when Jesus, after learning of their brother's terminal illness, chose to stay put for a couple of days (John 11:6). The disciples must have felt it when He attempted to pass them by as He walked over the stormy sea (Mark 6:48). And what about all those oppressed and struggling Jews who couldn't understand why Jesus, the focal point of their messianic hopes and dreams, so consistently resisted their attempts to lift Him to the throne (John 6:15)? Why did He allow His enemies to arrest Him, mock Him, and nail Him to a cross? Didn't He know that there are more practical and productive ways of setting up a kingdom?

Hindsight is always twenty-twenty, of course. The people who *lived* these biblical scenarios couldn't possibly have foreseen the plot twists that would bring their personal conflicts to resolution. They didn't understand that Lazarus was going to walk out of the tomb or that Jesus would calm the sea. They didn't expect the crucified Christ to rise again. Like the Jerusalem church, they had no way of knowing that, even as they prayed for his release, the apostle Peter would knock at their door (Acts 12:5-17).

Or did they?

Perhaps they *should* have known. Perhaps they should have realized that our Lord is too big, too creative, and too original to be confined within the narrow limits of human expectation. Maybe they should have allowed experience to teach them that God is not merely sovereign—He is sovereign *and* strange.

REFLECTION

Expect help where you least expect it.

DIVINE REVELRY

✳

"Euan, eu~oi~oi~oi~oi!"

The woods, the flowering meadows, even the sky rang with the wild, haunting, exhilarating cry. Lucy and Susan yielded themselves up to the sweetness of its triumphant music, clinging happily to the thick, dark fur of Aslan's mane. Cool fragrant air buffeted their cheeks and whipped their hair about their faces as the Lion sped relentlessly onward.

"I say, Lu," shouted Susan over the songs and laughter of the creatures running at their side, "do you suppose this can be his way of taking us into battle?"

But Lucy couldn't answer. She was completely caught up

in the rush and sweep of the hilarious, careening procession that they were leading over the dewy Narnian countryside. Never in her life had she known anything like it. It was pure intoxication.

"*Euan, eu-oi!*" Off to the left she saw Bacchus, the wild-eyed, skin-clad youth, dancing amid his lovely, loose-haired Maenads, an expression on his smooth, ruddy face as innocent as a babe's and as fierce as a brooding thundercloud's. On her right skipped Fauns and satyrs with bushy-tailed squirrels and long-eared rabbits scampering in and out between their cloven feet. In the rear raced a pack of barking dogs, prancing horses, shouting children, and brightly darting butterflies and birds.

"It *is* a romp, isn't it, Aslan?" sang Bacchus, brandishing his vine-covered thyrsus and tilting his glowing face up to the burning sky.

"More than that," replied the Lion. "It's a holiday. It's a Jubilee!"

"*Eu-oi-oi-oi-oi!*" answered Bacchus, while fat old Silenus raised a cup in tribute to the Lion and went tumbling backward over his donkey's tail.

Lucy couldn't help laughing aloud. What a day it had been! Once more she pictured to herself the march of the trees, their long, leafy limbs lashing the air as they headed off to battle. Again she recalled the wonder of the river god's reedy ascent and the swiftness with which Bacchus's ivy vines had engulfed the bridge and brought it crumbling down into the churning green water. She remembered how the wild-flowers had spread before them like fire. She giggled at the thought of the barefoot children who came dancing after them as they passed a gray school yard in the town.

These pleasant thoughts were interrupted by the Lion's roar. "And now, dear children," cried Aslan, gathering himself for one final great leap, "prepare yourselves, for victory is at hand! Open your eyes and behold the defeat of your enemies!"

With that the music, the singing, and the laughter mounted to the clouds. Together the Old Narnians surged forward like a mighty crashing wave. Lucy opened her eyes just in time to see King Miraz's soldiers throwing down their weapons. The battle was over.

*   *   *   *   *

One of the most incriminating charges to be leveled against the church during its two-millennium history is the accusation that it has taken the sweet, heady elixir of the Good News and turned it into a dry and dreary dogma. Many non-believers have come to take the dullness of the faithful few for granted. As a result, stereotypes like the Killjoy Christian, the Moralizing Methodist, and the Prune-Faced Puritan have become all too familiar in Western art, fiction, and drama—tiresomely, monotonously familiar.

It's easy to get incensed over this and raise a loud fuss about antireligious bias in the media. But there are moments when one can't help wondering whether the finger of blame should be pointed in the other direction. Where, after all, did the stereotypes come from? If we're honest, we'll have to admit that they weren't spontaneously generated in a vacuum. To an appreciable extent, Christians really have succeeded in making Christianity sterile, joyless, and boring.

C. S. Lewis did not find it so. Indeed, it was largely the stimulating, scintillating thrill of the biblical message—what G. K. Chesterton called "the romance of faith"—that captured Jack's heart and drew him into the fold. The further he traveled down the hedged and narrow road of atheism, Lewis said, the more intoxicating became the alluring scent of "joy" that was wafted to him from the open fields of Christian orthodoxy. That scent, as encountered in the authors he read—Malory and Langland, Herbert and Donne, MacDonald and Chesterton—and in the lives of the believers he knew—Paul Benecke, Hugo Dyson, J. R. R. Tolkien—ultimately proved irresistible. Even while an unconvinced agnostic, he was eventually led to confess, "Christians are wrong, but all the rest are bores."[33]

That perspective comes through clearly in his own writing. It surfaces again and again in *The Chronicles of Narnia.* It's especially strong in the account of Aslan's triumphant advance upon the Telmarine army at the head of a crowd of cavorting animals, dancing Fauns, and laughing, singing children. What we have here is a striking picture of the overwhelming, conquering power of unrestrained joy—a striking visual image of an idea Jack Lewis considered fundamental to the faith: the idea that life in Christ is meant to be a happy, holy revel.

You will show me the path of life;
In Your presence is fullness of joy;
At Your right hand are pleasures forevermore. (PSALM 16:11)

Holy revelry. *Divine* revelry. Here is a concept that bland believers need desperately to rediscover. What might the church be like, what kind of impact could it have upon the watching world, if we were to recall, in deed as well as in word, that life in God's kingdom is supposed to be a celebration, a festival, a wedding feast? David danced with abandon before the Lord (2 Samuel 6:14). Imagine what would happen if Christians were to do the same! Nonbelievers could criticize and laugh as much as they like. They certainly couldn't accuse us of being dull.

Has your Christian faith become boring? If so, remember that it was Jesus who compared the life-giving energy of the new covenant to the fizzing effervescence of fermentation (Matthew 9:17). This is the same Jesus who was known to frequent parties and who on one occasion even turned water into wine (John 2:1-11). Among His detractors He had the reputation of being a drunkard and a glutton (Matthew 11:19). Since that time, He has been celebrated in song as

"The Lord of the Dance"[34]—that "Great Dance" which, according to Lewis, guides the movements of the universe and orders the events of our daily lives.[35]

It's not by accident that Bacchus (or Dionysus), the Hellenic god of wine and conviviality, played a major role in this episode. To the ancient Greeks, Bacchus was a symbol of *life* in all its potency and fullness. Lewis imported him into the story and reworked him according to a Narnian design for a very good reason. He wanted to show us the wild and unpredictable side of grace. He was trying to give us a more vibrant appreciation of "energy, fertility, and urgency; the resource, the triumph, and even the insolence of things that grow."[36] It's in this sense that the Narnian Bacchus became yet another symbol of the Savior who proclaimed, "I have come that they may have life, and that they may have it more abundantly" (John 10:10).

Life more abundant. A life bubbling and exploding with excitement, vitality, and joy. Revelry—divine, holy revelry. Should it surprise us to find the Christian experience described in these terms? Not in the least. For as Lewis remarked in *Miracles,* Jesus "is the reality behind the false god Bacchus."[37]

REFLECTION

God's Kingdom is like a wild and wonderful romp.

"Then the lion said—but I don't know if it spoke—You will have to let me undress you. I was afraid of his claws, I can tell you, but I was pretty nearly desperate now. So I just lay flat down on my back to let him do it."

—THE VOYAGE OF THE "DAWN TREADER,"
CHAPTER 7, "HOW THE ADVENTURE ENDED"

A CHANGE OF CLOTHES

※

Up the steep mountainside toiled Eustace, the reluctant dragon, following the mysterious golden Lion. The arm-ring he'd taken from the dragon hoard bit deeply into the scaly skin and flesh of his left foreleg. At every step a searing pain shot up over his shoulder and across his back like a white-hot bolt of lightning. The loathsome bulk of his body and tail weighed him down like a ball and chain. If only it were possible to undo what had been done! If only he could go back to being a boy!

At the top of the mountain he cast a tentative glance at the Lion, sat back on his dragon haunches, and stared. There among the sharp rocks and scrubby pines was the last thing he'd expected to find in that barren place: a garden of fragrant fruit trees, and in its midst a wide, round pool with shining marble steps going down into it. Starlight glittered on the surface of the water, and Eustace suddenly felt certain that the pain in his leg would be eased if only he could plunge it into that crystal bath. He got up and made a move towards the pool.

Not yet, said a voice.

Eustace paused. He turned. Had the Lion really spoken? *First you must undress.*

But what did it mean, *undress?* Could it be that dragons, like snakes and lizards, cast their skins? Eager to get down into the glassy water, Eustace began scratching and clawing at himself. Soon his entire skin came peeling away, all in a single piece. He slipped it off and lumbered down to the pool.

At the top of the steps he paused and stretched out a toe. How could it be? His foot was as hard and as scaly as ever! Hadn't he stripped himself of that ugly hide? *Perhaps dragon skins*, he reflected, *come off in layers—like onion skins.* He stepped back and started clawing again.

But it was no good. Three times the skin sheered away as quick and as clean as a banana peel. Three times Eustace crawled to the water's edge only to find himself unchanged. In spite of all his efforts, his body remained as rough and reptilian as a crocodile's. *If I have to undress first*, he thought, *I'll never get into the water!*

Then the voice spoke again. *You will have to let* me *undress you*, it said.

You? thought Eustace, looking up at the Lion. He trembled at the sight of those terrible claws. He whimpered, and a plume of dark smoke floated up from his dragon nostrils. Then, in a gesture of utter despair, he flopped down on his back, stuck his legs straight up into the air, and lay there, absolutely motionless.

The Lion crouched; the Lion pounced. Eustace nearly fainted as he felt its knifelike claws piercing him to the heart. And then, in an instant, he was splashing in the water, rising into the night air, and standing before the majestic beast.

Eustace looked down. He was a boy again!

And he was dressed in a brand-new suit of Narnian clothes.

* * * * *

Despite the claims of the positive thinkers and motivational speakers, there *is* such a thing as a problem that defies human resolution. Live long enough and you will run up against an obstacle that simply *cannot* be overcome by pure self-will and determination.

It was in Narnia that this truth came home to Eustace Scrubb. In Narnia he awoke one starlit night only to make a terrifying discovery. He'd become a dragon, a repulsive, red-eyed, fire-breathing dragon, and he hadn't the slightest idea how to undo the nightmarish transformation.

Eustace's stint as a dragon is perhaps one of the best-loved and most oft-rehearsed episodes in *The Chronicles of Narnia*. And not without good reason: At some level every reader knows what it's like to be in Eustace's shoes . . . or scales.

Our predicament, like Eustace's, is at once far more basic *and* far more complex than the occasional technical difficulty or bump in the road. It's a question of who we are and what we've become, the nasty, clinging embarrassment of what the Bible calls the "old man"—the inescapable, unconquerable obstacle of our own sin nature.

Sin. It's not the theological abstraction many take it to be. Nor is it always the public enormity that calls so much attention to itself in headlines about war, murder, rape, or corporate scandal. Far more often it's as close to us as our own skin; as quiet, comfortable, and inconspicuous as a dirty old shirt or a worn-out pair of shoes.

Consider the sin of hatred. The term *hate*, in modern society, has been given a political definition. It's represented as a matter of rivalry between competing social groups. But hate, in actuality, is something far more personal, far more obstinate, and far more difficult to resolve than any political or social phenomenon, as is clear from this bitter confession from a humanitarian doctor in Dostoevsky's *The Brothers Karamazov:*

> "In my dreams," he said, "I have often come to making enthusiastic schemes for the service of humanity . . .

and yet I am incapable of living in the same room with anyone for two days together, as I know by experience. As soon as anyone is near me, his personality disturbs my self-complacency and restricts my freedom. In twenty-four hours I begin to hate the best of men: one because he's too long over his dinner; another because he has a cold and keeps on blowing his nose."[38]

"What's to be done?" asks the character to whom this story is told. "What can one do in such a case? Must one despair?" *That* is the ten-million-dollar question.

"Can the Ethiopian change his skin or the leopard its spots?" asked the prophet (Jeremiah 13:23). Can the boy-turned-dragon simply slough off the hard rind of his conceit and selfish, dragonish thoughts? Not likely. Not short of a miracle.

A miracle was what Eustace needed. And a miracle is exactly what he got—once he was *desperate* enough to receive it. When with much fear he had tried and failed to rid himself of the curse, only then did he hear the voice of the Lion offering him the solution: *You will have to let* me *undress you.*

It's here that Eustace's story jumps off the page and confronts us with a breathtaking promise. When you've come to the realization that you can't do it yourself, take heart: *There is Someone else who can do it for you.*

*O wretched man that I am! Who will deliver me from this body
of death? I thank God—through Jesus Christ our Lord!*

(ROMANS 7:24-25)

Christ, like the great Lion Aslan, stands waiting in the wings,
ready to strip away the ugly hide of the hateful old self. He is
able to wash away your sin—not just in an academic, theoreti-
cal, or theological sense, but in the experiential here and now.
As the heavenly Father clothed our shamed and fallen first
parents (Genesis 3:21), even so will He cleanse and clothe
you.

> *When He shall come with trumpet sound,*
> *Oh, may I then in Him be found;*
> *Dressed in His righteousness alone,*
> *Faultless to stand before the throne.*[39]

It won't necessarily be easy. It may, as in Eustace's case, hurt
"like billy-oh." But the end result will be a thing of incompa-
rable beauty: new garments of the purest white, a change of
clothes reserved for those whose names are written in the
Lamb's Book of Life (Revelation 3:5).

REFLECTION

God helps those who are desperate for a change.

At first it looked like a cross, then it looked like an aeroplane, then it looked like a kite, and at last with a whirring of wings it was right overhead and was an albatross.

—THE VOYAGE OF THE "DAWN TREADER," CHAPTER 12, "THE DARK ISLAND"

THE SIGN OF THE ALBATROSS

❋

Arrow on string, Lucy leaned heavily against the fighting-top rail, listening to the murmurs of the archers on either side of her. She could see their strained faces in the glow of the lamp that hung from the mast above their heads. She could sense their fear.

Up from the deck drifted the voices of crewmen huddled in the darkness below: "We'll never get out," muttered some. "We're rowing in circles," grumbled others.

The air was deathly still. Neither sail nor banner nor hem of cloak stirred as the rowers drove the *Dawn Treader* deeper into shadow. Lucy could see the sailor Rynelf at the prow, peering into the blackness beyond the ship's carved figure-head. In the light of the stern's lantern she caught a glimpse of Caspian whispering intently to Lord Drinian, his brow creased with anxiety.

Suddenly the silence was split by a piercing laugh. "Never get out!" shrieked the wild-looking stranger the crew had rescued from the sea. Lucy shuddered at the harsh, grating sound of his voice. "No, no! They'll never let me go that easily!"

After that, the darkness grew even deeper. It seemed to close in around the ship like a smothering blanket. Eerie sounds rose out of the surrounding deep. Forgotten night-mares forced their way up out of Lucy's subconscious mind and gamboled mockingly in the air before her. She squeezed her eyes shut and tried to block them out.

"Aslan," she whispered, bowing her head. "Aslan, if you love us, send us help now!"

It wasn't an instant later that she heard the voice of Rynelf lifted in a shout. "Ho! Look there! Just off the starboard bow!"

Lucy raised her eyes. In the sky ahead burned a bright speck, like a tiny glowing star. Slowly it grew and approached until it hung just above the ship. In the next moment a broad beam of light fell from it, setting the *Dawn Treader's* green and gold embellishments blazing against the surrounding blackness. Lucy squinted into the glare and saw a spot of brighter brilliance emerging in its midst, like a flame in the form of a flying cross. As she watched, this flame resolved itself into the shape of a soaring seabird—a great white albatross. She could hear the sweep of its wings as it circled the mast three times. She trembled as it drew near and whispered to her in a voice like the voice of Aslan. "Courage, dear heart!" was all it said.

From the masthead the albatross descended to the prow, where it perched momentarily upon the ship's carved dragon head. Then, after emitting a strong, sweet cry, it took to the air again.

"Steer after it, my lord Drinian!" called Caspian. "Surely it intends us good!"

And so it was. For as the *Dawn Treader* followed the miraculous bird, the darkness gradually lightened until at last the ship burst out into open daylight.

From the fighting-top, Lucy glanced over her shoulder at the shrinking black smudge behind the stern. She sighed, leaned back against the mast, and wiped her eyes.

"Thank you," she whispered. "Thank you, *Aslan.*"

*   *   *   *   *

It's arguable that *The Voyage of the "Dawn Treader"* is the most richly symbolic piece of writing C. S. Lewis ever produced. Symbolism is present throughout his work, of course—in his poetry, for instance, or the ever popular Space Trilogy,[40] or his autobiographical allegory, *The Pilgrim's Regress.*[41] But there's a difference here. In some ways, it's the difference between the subtle shadings of a Rembrandt painting and the leaping colors of a medieval illuminated text. *Dawn Treader* fairly pops with vibrant and deeply meaningful visual imagery. In this instance, Lewis's accolade for Tolkien's *The Lord of the Rings* seems applicable to his own work: "Here are beauties which pierce like swords and burn like cold iron."[42]

Some of the book's most haunting and enchanting visions are those that cluster around the *Dawn Treader's* narrow escape from the ominous Dark Island (chapter 12). At the center of this memorable constellation of word pictures shines a striking image of the power of truth and hope: that of a single ray of light piercing the darkness. And in the midst of this beam of illumination hovers what may be the most mysterious and compelling figure of all: the great seabird, the albatross, who arrives in answer to Lucy's prayer, comforts her with the voice of Aslan, and guides the ship out of the murk and into the light of day.

It's not by chance that Lewis chose the albatross to play the role of deliverer in this scene. As it happens, there is a long literary tradition of Christian symbolism associated with this particular bird. Seafaring men of old held it in great awe and regarded it as a messenger from God. Its appearance in the sky was always interpreted as an omen of great good.

"I remember the first albatross I ever saw," writes Herman Melville in *Moby Dick:* "At intervals it arched forth its vast archangel wings, as if to embrace some holy ark. . . . Through its inexpressible, strange eyes, methought I peeped to secrets not below the heavens. As Abraham before the angels, I bowed myself."[43]

Melville's reverential feelings toward the bird hark back to Samuel Taylor Coleridge's famous "The Rime of the Ancient Mariner," a strange and surreal poetic odyssey that gets underway as an albatross guides a distressed ship out of a deadly ice storm:

> At length did cross an Albatross:
> Thorough the fog it came;
> As if it had been a Christian soul,
> We hailed it in God's name.[44]

But Coleridge takes the imagery even further in the direction of specifically *Christian* symbolism. For when the fictional narrator of the story commits the unthinkable crime by *murdering* the albatross—"the bird that loved the man who shot him with his bow"[45]—he is forced, by way of punishment, to hang its body around his neck "instead of the cross."[46] The meaning could hardly be clearer. In some sense or other, the Ancient Mariner's albatross is a picture of Christ, the harmless and innocent Son of God, who, for the sake of love, died at the hands of those He came to deliver.

Lewis must surely have had this kind of symbolism in mind when he introduced an albatross into the story of the

Dawn Treader. This is why the bird first appears to Lucy in the shape of a cross and descends to the ship at the center of a heaven-sent beam of light, light which, though it "does not alter the surrounding darkness," is nevertheless sufficient to illumine the *Dawn Treader* and save everyone on board. This is why the albatross tenderly draws near to Lucy and speaks to her in the voice of Aslan himself. In every detail the great seabird is an image of Jesus, the Light of the World (John 8:12; 9:5), the Savior who swoops unhesitatingly to our rescue in answer to heartfelt prayer.

The message is as heartening as it is simple: When in darkness, breathe out a prayer for help. The light that comes in answer, be it ever so small, will always be enough to dispel the deepest shadows. For at the heart of that narrow beam burns an unmistakable image of hope, the sign of the Deliverer, rising in the form of the cross.

REFLECTION

Christ Himself is the light in our darkness.

"*Travellers who have come from far to Aslan's Table,*" said the girl. "*Why do you not eat and drink?*"

—*THE VOYAGE OF THE "DAWN TREADER,"* CHAPTER 13, "THE THREE SLEEPERS"

PERILOUS TABLE

❋

Edmund squinted through the gloaming down the length of the massive table. Silver flasks and cut crystal goblets glinted in the starlight, bright against the backdrop of the deep crimson cloth. His stomach growled and his right eyebrow twitched. *What a miserable way to spend a night,* he thought. *Empty bellies, mounds of food, and we dare not touch a single morsel!*

He'd been skeptical all along, of course—since the moment the crew of the *Dawn Treader* had set foot on the mysterious island. Glancing now from the faces of his nodding and drowsing companions to the flagons of red wine, heaps of brown bread, and plates of steaming roast meat, he suddenly knew why. *This is all just too good to be true.*

Yes, that was it. The rich food, the tantalizing scents, the inviting softness of the island itself—it was enough to raise the suspicions of the thickest dullard on earth. After all, how often does one come across a banquet in the middle of a deserted island? The whole situation smelled of magic and enchantment.

Caspian and the others agreed, of course. Together they had come to the conclusion that the three men sleeping at the head of the table must be under the spell of the bewitched food. And so they had determined to keep watch all through the night, withholding their hands from the sumptuous feast, in an attempt to solve the mystery of the place. But they had chosen their seats at the perilous table with meticulous care.

Edmund yawned. Then he rubbed his eyes, opened them wide, and peered again into the darkness.

But what was this? Not far away, just beyond the shaggy gray shapes of the three enchanted sleepers, a point of light, like a tiny star, had appeared. He saw now what it was: the flame of a candle set in a tall silver candlestick. And holding the candlestick was the loveliest young woman he had ever beheld.

Lucy, Eustace, Caspian, and Reepicheep saw her too. Edmund knew this, for as if by unspoken consent they all rose to greet her. Gracefully she approached them, the hem of her blue robe sweeping the dew from the grass. Then with her free hand she smoothed the yellow hair back from her forehead, gazed at them out of violet eyes, and spoke:

"Is the food not to your liking?"

Out of the corner of one eye, Edmund could see the others fidgeting. With a great effort, he found his tongue and answered her. "Please—we thought it was accursed."

She smiled. In that moment Edmund knew that she could not be a witch.

"Accursed?" she said. "Oh no, my friends! For this is *Aslan's* Table. It is set here in his honor for the sustenance of all who travel so far. Eat freely of it! Only thus will you be nourished and find strength to reach your journey's end."

*   *   *   *   *

"Take, eat."

With these two words Jesus instituted the only formal ceremony He ever bequeathed to His fledgling church. It was a move of revolutionary simplicity on His part. In place of the rituals of the pagans and the sacrifices of the Old Testament law, He established the observance of a plain, common meal. He called His followers together around an ordinary table, where He broke the bread and poured the wine, then offered them to His friends, saying, "Take. Eat. Drink. This is My body and My blood, freely given for you. Do this in remembrance of Me."[47]

"Why do you not eat and drink?" asks Ramandu's daughter when she finds the five travelers sitting at Aslan's Table, trembling in the predawn darkness and cold. The answer, of course, is that they are afraid: afraid of the unknown, the unexplainable, the uncontrollable.

C. S. Lewis was well-acquainted with such doubts, fears, and misgivings. As an atheist, young Jack was repulsed by everything that had to do with the Christian faith. Later, as an intellectual rationally convinced of the truth of the gospel, he embraced the *doctrines* of the church but still struggled to overcome an aversion to some of its *sacraments*, especially the Lord's Supper. Why? He explains in one of his *Letters to Malcolm:*

> Some people seem able to discuss different theories of this act as if they understood them all and needed only evidence as to which was best. This light has been withheld from me. I do not know and can't imagine what the disciples understood Our Lord to mean when, His body still unbroken and His blood unshed, He handed them the bread and wine, saying they were His body and blood.[48]

"I do not know and can't imagine. . . ." In other words, Lewis, the brilliant Oxford don, had trouble wrapping his *mind* around the marvel of Holy Communion; and having been trained as a rationalist, he was naturally apprehensive about anything he couldn't logically explain. Where this particular aspect of the Christian life is concerned, he seems to have felt very much as Edmund did about the magical food on Aslan's Table: skeptical and suspicious . . . perhaps even scared.

We shouldn't blame him for this. There is good reason to approach the Lord's Table with a measure of fear. Like the one Edmund and his friends discovered on Ramandu's island, this table is perilous. It's perilous because it conceals a profound *mystery*. Something happens at this table that no one can quite explain. Here, as we "take and eat," we enter into union with the Christ who said, "I am the living bread which came down from heaven. If anyone eats of this bread, he will live forever" (John 6:51).

Exactly *how* this happens—the "mechanics" of the operation, so to speak—is a question beyond the scope of human understanding. Just about every scholar has tried to answer it. Still, to make such an attempt is to threaten the sense of wonder that is so essential to experiencing the miracle of the table. At least that's how Jack came to see it. "I am not saying to anyone in the world, 'Your explanation is wrong.' I am saying, 'Your explanation leaves the mystery for me still a mystery,'" he said.[49]

And so it should. Perhaps this is why, in *The Voyage of the "Dawn Treader,"* Lewis has given us such a highly imaginative and hauntingly beautiful picture of a table at the edge of the world, a table of perpetual bounty where a feast is renewed daily for the benefit of weary travelers. Perhaps he wanted to plant in the reader's mind a hint of the joy and awe with which we should approach the table where Jesus broke the bread and poured the wine. Surely it was this sense of wonder and romance that brought about the change in his own attitude toward Holy Communion over the years:

> At first Jack followed his childhood practice of receiving communion only on great holidays, such as Christmas and Easter, but before long he wrote to Warren that receiving communion once a month was a good compromise between being Laodicean and enthusiastic. . . . But in the last fifteen or so years of his life, I think he normally received communion every week.[50]

"Why do you not eat and drink?" Is it because, like the young Jack Lewis, you fear that which you cannot logically explain? Or are you, like Edmund, distrustful of a grace so bountiful that it seems too good to be true? If so, it may be time to try another approach. Step up to the table, *take, and eat.* "Oh, taste and see that the Lord is good" (Psalm 34:8).

Only thus will you be nourished and find strength to reach your journey's end.

REFLECTION

God sustains us in the mystery of the Lord's Table.

> "[One of your company] must go on
> into the utter east and never return into
> the world."
>
>   "That is my heart's desire," said
> Reepicheep.

—*THE VOYAGE OF THE "DAWN TREADER,"* CHAPTER 14,
"THE BEGINNING OF THE END OF THE WORLD."

HEART'S DESIRE

❋

It was all so very like a dream—a dream too beautiful to be real and too real to be a dream at all. The brightness of the light suffused their bodies with a sense of vibrant calm. The colors in the sky were hard and sharp enough to pierce the eye. An intense, pervasive hush hung palpably over the shimmering whiteness of the Silver Sea.

Up rose the sun, a flashing iridescent disc riding above the blue-green sea wave that trembled on the horizon. Lucy watched in silence as Reepicheep, his glossy, black fur gleaming in the sunrise, stood up in the bows of the boat and began lowering his little coracle into the lily-covered water.

"This," she heard him say, "is where I go on alone."

Without thinking, she got up to help him. Edmund and Eustace did the same. Of course he must go on alone. It had long since been decided. On into Aslan's country, that great, green, pine-clad, mountainous country rising endlessly above and beyond the sun's flame. That, she knew, was what the Mouse wanted more than anything. She remembered what he had told them about his infancy and the Dryad's cradle song:

Where sky and water meet,
Where the waves grow sweet,
Doubt not, Reepicheep,
To find all you seek,
There is the utter East.[51]

Deftly Reepicheep loosed his rapier and drew it from his belt, bright as the morning star. In one graceful motion he flung it out in a golden arc over the water. Far away they could see it now, its jeweled hilt standing upright among the lilies. "I shall need it no more," he said as he turned to face his companions.

Lucy stood looking down at the valiant Mouse through tears. Though so small, he had a heart as great as any champion's. Though so fierce, he was yet tender enough to be infinitely susceptible to whispers of beauty from beyond the edge of the world. Touched by that tenderness, she yielded at last to a wish that had been present at the back of her mind ever since the day she met him: Bending low, she embraced him and stroked his thick, soft fur.

She would have held him longer, but he broke away. Without a word he leapt from the boat into the bobbing coracle. Not once did he look back, but paddled straight through the mass of undulating white blossoms, up the steep green wave, down the other side, and on into the glare of the sun. The last they saw of him was the feather atop his head, dipping and nodding in circles against the light.

"I asked him once," said Lucy, watching him go, "whether he thought Aslan's country would be the sort of country you could ever sail to."

"I remember," said Edmund. "I suppose he knows the answer by now."

"Yes," she said quietly after a pause. "Thanks to him, we all do."

*   *   *   *   *

Of the many themes Jack Lewis explored during his lifelong career as a writer, speaker, teacher, and storyteller, that of *desire* is perhaps the most persistent and omnipresent. It pops up everywhere—in his novels, his sermons, his books on Christian doctrine, his works of criticism. It was central not only to his literary labors but to the way he lived and understood his personal life. It's also one of the golden threads that runs through *The Chronicles of Narnia* from beginning to end.

We've already touched upon this subject in our reflection on Digory, the Witch, and the apple ("All Get What They Want"). We will have occasion to visit it again before our tour of the land of Narnia is done. But for the moment we want to pay special attention to the powerful role desire plays in the adventures of one of Lewis's most engaging characters: Reepicheep the Mouse.

The story of Reepicheep is the story of a desire-driven life. This remarkable rodent, so bold in battle, so refined in the art of courtesy, so fervent and faithful in every enterprise, has a secret fire burning in his breast. Almost from infancy he has known that he was born to be a seeker. His entire existence is a quest. As the tale of *The Voyage of the "Dawn Treader"* unfolds, we watch with a kind of awe as that quest leads him step-by-step to the place where he is destined to "find all he seeks": the End of the World and Aslan's country itself.

Is it any wonder that the Mouse's personality can be uncomfortably intense at times? Eustace—at least at the beginning of the voyage—thinks Reepicheep arrogant and stuck-up. Rhince and Drinian (in the adventure of "The Dark Island") find him rash and foolhardy. Even King Caspian is eventually compelled to cry, "Will no one silence that Mouse?"[52] But it's all because Reepicheep refuses to swerve either to the right or the left. His hopes, goals, and purposes are higher than those of his companions—"as high as [his] spirit"[53]—and they completely dominate his outlook and determine all his actions.

Jesus was looking for "a few good men" with this kind of vision when He came calling disciples by the shores of Galilee. Unfortunately, many of His would-be followers failed to measure up to Reepicheep's standard of devotion:

And another also said, "Lord, I will follow You, but let me first go and bid them farewell who are at my house." But Jesus said to him, "No one, having put his hand to the plow, and looking back, is fit for the kingdom of God." (LUKE 9:61-62)

Reepicheep never looked back. Danger and disappointment could not dissuade him. Fond embraces and tearful farewells could not hold him. His sights were set upon a goal that lay beyond the boundaries of the world. Like those Old Testament saints who confessed themselves "strangers and pilgrims on the earth," he desired "a better, that is, a heavenly country" (Hebrews 11:13, 16).

In all of this, the courtly Mouse is a model of the true Christian disciple: the man or woman who says to God, "Whom have I in heaven but You? And there is none upon earth that I desire besides You" (Psalm 73:25). Like Reepicheep, such disciples understand that they were *born* to seek the prize: perfect fellowship with the Lord of life in the land of deathless light. What's more, they are convinced that *everything* depends upon success. To achieve the quest is to gain the whole world; to fail is to lose their own soul.

But failure is not an option. For those who go questing in

the spirit of Reepicheep, a hopeful end is assured. As the Mouse teaches us, we *can* sail to Aslan's country if only we will embark in the right boat and hold our course steady till the end. God Himself has promised it:

Then you will call upon Me and go and pray to Me, and I will listen to you. And you will seek Me and find Me, when you search for Me with all your heart. (JEREMIAH 29:12-13)

"A desire," wrote Lewis in *Surprised by Joy*, "is turned not to itself but to its object. . . . It is the object that makes the desire itself desirable or hateful."[54] Herein lies the difference between Reepicheep and all those who "get what they want but don't like it." The end he pursues, like the longing that drives him, is good and true. He is a creature of single vision; in other words, his heart is pure. And as the Bible tells us more than once, the pure heart receives what it desires (Psalm 37:4): It is enabled to *see God* (Matthew 5:8).

REFLECTION

The undeflected heart reaches the goal.

"But really, we can only ask him."

—*THE SILVER CHAIR*, CHAPTER I, "BEHIND THE GYM"

ONLY ASK

✳

Jill had never really liked him. She hadn't even known him very well until he discovered her crying behind the gym. That's when *everything* started to change.

"I say, Pole," he'd said, strolling up to her with his hands in his pockets. "What's up?" And she, of course, had flown into a rage. After all, what girl wants a boy to catch her blubbering? Especially a boy with a name like Eustace Scrubb.

Now she was sitting, chin in hands, listening to the soft drone of his voice. Why was he being so nice to her? He seemed to understand about *Them* and their incessant bullying. He even tried to console her with a peppermint. Sucking the candy thoughtfully, she began paying closer attention to what he was saying.

That's when it hit her.

Eustace was talking nonsense. Telling her crazy things. Things about a place "outside the world," a place where fairy tales come true and where *They* can't torment you. A place you can get to only by means of Magic.

She turned on him fiercely. "Now you're making fun of me!" she said.

"No, no!" protested Eustace, blushing. "I know what you must be thinking. But it's all true! We were just whisked away! And—well, I've been wondering . . ."

"Wondering what?"

"Wondering if we could make it happen again. I was thinking that you, of all people, might be interested in . . . finding *a way out.*"

Jill squinted up at him. "What do *you* know about Magic, anyway? Are you talking about spells and charms? Circles on the ground and that sort of thing?"

He frowned. "I *had* considered that type of magic. But now I have a feeling that he wouldn't much like it. Somehow I think he'd prefer that we just *ask* him."

"Ask who?"

"Aslan, of course. At least that's what they call him there."

Aslan. Jill trembled at the name in spite of herself. In the next moment she heard a sound—footsteps approaching from the other side of the gym! She turned and looked Eustace in the eye.

"All right," she whispered, her heart pounding like a drum. "Let's do it!"

They held out their arms and faced east, looking up the hill through the laurels to the wall that surrounded Experiment House.

"Repeat after me," said Eustace. "Aslan! Aslan!"

"Aslan," murmured Jill, following his lead. "We ask you to let us go into . . ."

The footsteps were drawing nearer. A cry rang out: "She's back there!"

"It's *Them!*" hissed Eustace. "Run! Perhaps the door in the wall is open!"

Up the slope they ran then, panting and sweating, scraping their hands and faces against the tree branches, until they reached the wall. Jill's heart sank; the door was shut! But in the next moment Eustace's hand was on the latch, and then the latch was turning. In swung the door on its rusty, creaking hinges. Instantly a ray of blinding sunshine and a flash of bright blue sky burst through from the other side.

"Come on!" said Eustace, squeezing her hand. "*This is it!*"

* * * * *

How does one get to the land of Narnia? So far, we've seen this question answered in a couple of different ways. On at least two occasions the Pevensies have landed there by "accident," by stumbling into a wardrobe and falling through a picture. They've also been "pulled" or "drawn" into the otherworld by the power of an irresistible call. Different stories, different circumstances, and yet in each of these instances the role our heroes and heroines have played in the entry process has been almost entirely *passive.*

In *The Silver Chair,* Lewis took another tack. What might happen, he asked, if someone were to assume a more active approach? If he or she were to *try* to get into Narnia by way of conscious, deliberate effort? What if someone were to seize the initiative rather than wait for the adventure to "happen"?

It's a question of huge significance at the dawn of the twenty-first century—the kind of question increasing numbers of our contemporaries are asking every day. For as it turns out, the so-called postmodern era has at least this one great spiritual advantage over the more rationalistic and scientific age that preceded it: Today, more people actually believe in the existence of an Unseen Reality. And many of them are willing to do just about anything to get in touch with it.

How does one go about making contact with the spiritual world? What exactly should a person *do* if he or she wants to find the "Narnia" that lies on the other side of the door of humdrum, everyday life? Down through the ages, mankind has proposed and experimented with a wide variety of solutions to this problem. The answers have been as colorfully diverse as human culture itself. Religion, ritual, and sacrifice. Fasting, prayer, and meditation. Alms, vigils, and pilgrimages. *Magic.*

Magic. In a sense, it can be argued that this one method actually sums up and contains all the others within itself. For whatever their differences may be, all of these humanly conceived paths to the spiritual world share a single idea in common. Not only do they assure us that we *can* do something to reach the other side, they actually tell us exactly *what* that something is. Chant these words. Trace these symbols in the sand. Avoid these taboos. Kill this particular animal in this particular way. Read your Bible every day. Go to church on Sunday.

This, in a nutshell, is the *magical* worldview. It's the notion that the universe operates according to the rule of tit for tat. In essence, it claims that reality is mechanical and impersonal; that in the spiritual realm, as in the physical, laws of cause and effect are constant and invariable. A shove here creates a bulge there. Pushing button A produces result B. Swirl a concoction of herbs into his drink, and the man of your dreams will fall in love with you. Say "Alohomora" and the door will open. Repeat a prayer every night and you'll go to heaven. Always. Without exception. Regardless of your motives, background, or personal character. That's magic.

In the opening scene of *The Silver Chair,* Eustace told Jill that one could only get to Narnia by means of "magic." But the "magic" he had in mind was clearly something very different from the mechanistic methodologies described above. He was not thinking of the incantations, spells, and circle casting of traditional witchcraft and wizardry. How do we know this? Because when Jill suggested *that* option, Eustace rejected it. He called it all "rot." More importantly, he concluded that it probably wouldn't meet with Aslan's approval. Why not? Because "it would look as if we thought we could make him do things."[55]

What was Eustace's alternative? What sort of "magic" was he proposing? It's here that we come to the crux of the issue. For the answer he gave is not only thoroughly scriptural and Christian, it also has the effect of illuminating the fundamental distinction between the biblical worldview and all other spiritual perspectives. It shows us that, in the end, everything comes down to a simple choice. We can attempt to manipulate. Or we can throw ourselves in utter dependence upon sovereign grace. "Really," said Eustace, "we can only ask him."[56]

At the heart of the universe stands not a set of principles, but a Person. *He* is the door that leads to the other side (John 10:9). We can reach the place of our dreams and longings only in the context of *relationship* with Him. There is nothing—absolutely nothing—we can do to *make* it happen. We can only *ask.*

Ask, and it will be given to you; seek, and you will find; knock, and it will be opened to you. For everyone who asks receives, and he who seeks finds, and to him who knocks it will be opened. (MATTHEW 7:7-8)

Magic promises power, power to influence the course of the cosmos and to have our own will and way. Faith, by contrast, offers us communion with a wise and loving Father.

Which will *you* choose?

R E F L E C T I O N
The power of prayer lies in having a personal
relationship with God.

LION'S BREATH

✳

It was odd the way he made her feel, this golden-furred, dark-maned, honey-tongued Lion. Though she was terribly afraid of his claws, his teeth, and his relentlessly probing eyes, Jill took a strange comfort in the warmth and sweetness of his breath. Once or twice she wondered if he was only a vision, but in the long spaces between those few moments of madness she knew that nothing could be more solid or more real. No nightmare had ever been so terrifying, no dream so reassuring.

Never once did he raise his voice, and yet so great was the force of his mere presence that she was compelled to accord him her obedience and respect. When he asked her what had become of the boy Eustace, she realized that she could not skirt the truth and deny knowing that he'd fallen off the cliff. And when he proceeded to give her an assignment, she understood that refusal was not an option.

Her task? To seek the lost prince of Narnia, though it were to the uttermost ends of that world.

"But how," she asked, when at last he let her raise the question that had been burning in her mind all along, *"how do you expect me to get to Narnia in the first place?"*

"On my breath," he answered. "But let's not get ahead of ourselves. First you must turn and walk before me to the edge of the cliff."

To the edge of the cliff? But that was where Eustace had so lately fallen nearly to his ruin, where Jill had almost killed him by showing off and standing too near the precipice! *On my breath?* What could it possibly mean? The hair was rising along the back of her scalp; a cold dampness was gathering on her forehead. But it was no use. She had to do as he said. Slowly, submissively she turned and began walking toward the craggy verge.

"And now, Daughter of Eve," she heard him say, *"fare-well . . ."*

Already the golden voice was fading. Looking over her shoulder, she saw to her great surprise that the cliff face was already a great way behind her, melting into the hazy distance. Beneath her was nothing but air. She clapped a hand to her head. *Lion's breath!* she thought. *I'm floating on lion's breath!* It was like nothing so much as riding on a heap of fluffy down pillows. She closed her eyes and fell asleep. . . .

Jill awoke. Below her raced fleets of white clouds casting spotty shadows over an endless blue expanse: the sea! Slowly it heaved its wide bulk in great rhythmic ripples from horizon to horizon. Then she noticed that the clouds were rising to meet her: she was obviously descending at an alarming rate of speed. Gradually a wide band of dark green began to grow along the western edge of her vision. Land! And then there was a harbor filled with brightly colored ships and a many-turreted castle bedecked with flapping pennons and banners. Lower and lower she swooped until at last she was dropped down in the middle of a festive crowd gathered on the bank of a broad river. She looked up and there was Eustace, standing practically at her elbow.

"Well!" said Jill with a great sigh of relief. "Looks like I'm in Narnia at last!"

*　*　*　*　*

Imagine how Jill must have felt as she floated along far above the clouds. There was no sense of motion, no buffeting of the wind, no twisting or turning, no tumbling head over heels. Yet hours later she traversed a distance greater than that covered by the *Dawn Treader* during a voyage of many months. Her progress across the face of the world was swift and smooth, like a journey by jet airliner, only without the plane. More to the point, it was passive and effortless. That's what it's like to ride on a blast of lion's breath.

Episodes highlighting the power of Aslan's breath recur so often in the Narnia tales that they practically beg us to sit up and take notice. Time and time again when the great Lion opened his mouth and began to blow, the plot shifted, the tables turned, and events of strategic significance occurred. One can almost make the case that Aslan did nothing in these stories except by the efficacy of his breath.

In *The Magician's Nephew,* for instance, he created an entire world by breathing out a song.[57] In *The Lion, the Witch and the Wardrobe,* he convinced Susan and Lucy of the reality of his resurrection by "the warmth of his breath."[58] In the same book, he brought statues to life simply by exhaling upon them.[59] At the conclusion of *The Silver Chair,* he blew the whole world of Narnia away "like wreaths of smoke."[60] In *The Last Battle,* he roared and the stars fell from the sky.[61]

There is nothing, it seems, that the breath of Aslan could not do. It created and destroyed. It comforted, strengthened, and healed. It bestowed the gift of life. And in this tale, it raised Jill above the obstacles of the world and took her to a place where she could effectively set forth on the quest to which she had been called. It lifted her up, carried her, and enabled her to do her work.

In each of these particulars, Aslan's breath can hardly fail to remind us of the wonder-working might of the Spirit of God. In case after case, its mode of influence and methods of operation directly paralleled those of the "rushing mighty wind" that filled the upper room in Jerusalem on the day of Pentecost (Acts 2). After all, it was God's Spirit or *ruach* (Hebrew for "breath" or "wind") that "was hovering over the face of the waters" at creation (Genesis 1:2). It was the Spirit that breathed life into the nostrils of the man the Lord fashioned out of clay (Genesis 2:7). And it was the Spirit who, in Ezekiel's vision of the dry bones, revived the dead so that "breath came into them, and they lived, and stood upon their feet, an exceedingly great army" (Ezekiel 37:10). That vision concluded with a powerful promise:

"Then you shall know that I am the Lord, when I have opened your graves, O My people, and brought you up from your graves. I will put My Spirit in you, and you shall live, and I will place you in your own land. Then you shall know that I, the Lord, have spoken it and performed it," says the Lord. (EZEKIEL 37:13-14)

Lion's breath. In Lewis's mythology, it shaped worlds, strengthened failing hearts, and transformed figures of stone into bodies of living flesh. It bore Jill Pole to the land of Narnia and propelled her forward along a path of heroism and derring-do. In the same way, the breath of Yahweh—God's Holy Spirit—will lift us up, fill us with new vitality, place us in "our own land," and enable us to accomplish all our Master's will . . . *provided* we remain open and receptive to the influence of His gentle breathings.

As Jesus told His disciples at the Last Supper, "Without Me you can do nothing" (John 15:5).

That is why, as one of His last acts on earth, "He *breathed* on them, and said to them, 'Receive the Holy Spirit' " (John 20:22).

REFLECTION

The Spirit of God is the breath of life.

FOOT IN THE FIRE

❋

Thrum, thrum, thrum. Puddleglum's brain throbbed in sympathy with the gentle, pulsing rhythm of the mandolin. As he watched, the Witch's eyes, green and feline, expanded novalike until they filled his field of vision. Soft as a shadow she glided from one end of the room to the other, always keeping her pale and lovely face toward the Marsh-wiggle and his friends, her long white fingers endlessly stroking the silver strings.

Thrum, thrum, thrum. Thick and sweet the music hung upon the air—thick and sweet and palpable as the heavy smoke rising from the fire on the hearth. Puddleglum fidgeted. He crossed one webbed foot over the other and shifted his weight, then gritted his teeth and tried to turn away.

"It was all a dream," he heard her saying in soothing, sing-song tones. "There never was such a world as—how did you call it? Ah, yes—*Narnia*."

As if from a great distance, the dull, flat voices of Jill and Eustace reached his ear, echoing the dreadful words: "Never was such a world."

"Nor any sky," the Witch cooed, caressing her instrument as if it were a kitten, "nor sun nor stars. There never was such a person as *Aslan*."

Thrum, thrum, thrum. He felt as if his head were filled with molasses. A cloud of greenish fog appeared before his eyes. "No such person," repeated another voice, nearer at hand this time—could it have been his own?—"No such person as Aslan."

"And now to bed, dear friends," she concluded with a grim smile. "Tomorrow is another day. Let us have done with foolish dreams."

"Done," mumbled Jill and Eustace and Prince Rilian. "Done with dreams."

With a tortured effort Puddleglum wrenched his gaze from her face and turned to look at his companions. All three stood drooping like puppets unstrung, their eyes half-closed, chins upon their chests.

Thrum, thrum, thrum. "Soft pillows," she was chanting. "Sweet darkness. Dreamless sleep."

At that moment something stirred within him. A flame

flashed across his brain. Clenching his fists, he twisted his head to one side and strove to lift his leaden feet. Up came the left one; a bead of sweat trickled down his forehead. Up came the right. Mustering every ounce of his failing will and strength, Puddleglum fought against the sluggishness in his limbs, stubbornly inching his way towards the fire. At last he stood beside the hearth, right foot poised in midair. Then—

"Fool! Mud-filth!" she screeched. "Just *what* do you think you are doing?"

But it was too late. His foot was in the fire. With a shock of searing pain, the reality of their situation dawned upon him clear as day. Biting his lip and stifling a cry, he gave the coals a kick and scattered the burning fragments over the stones.

"A word with you, Madam," said Puddleglum as he came limping back.

* * * * *

Narnia was a country as subtly perilous as it was stunningly beautiful. Those who wanted to traverse this world of flowering hills, sunlit vales, glassy green seas, and hushed woods could never forget that dark enchantments lay in ambush at every turn. The traveler's safety hung in constant doubt. Everything depended upon his or her determination to *resist* evil.

Rilian, heir to the Narnian throne, failed to stand firm against one of these lurking bewitchments. As a result, he fell into bondage in the underground kingdom of the Emerald Witch. Eustace, Jill, and Puddleglum the Marsh-wiggle set out at Aslan's call to rescue the young prince. But it was an assignment far more demanding and difficult than any of them could have imagined; for the task could not be accomplished until they, too, had faced the enchantress's suggestive spells.

Marsh-wiggles, as every reader of *The Chronicles of Narnia* knows, are made of some very tough stuff. And it's a good thing they are. Because in the end it was Puddleglum—good old, gloomy old, cheerfully downbeat Puddleglum—who saved the day. He alone was stoical and stubborn enough to fight his way through the Witch's cloud of sweet green incense. Only he had the sober presence of mind to stick his foot in the fire and break her soporific spell. No one who has read Lewis's description of this simple act of defiance will ever forget it. It's one of the most magically symbolic moments in the entire history of Narnia.

Have you ever been in the Marsh-wiggle's position? Did you ever sit in the back row with an uneasy feeling while heads nodded in drowsy agreement with the noises coming from the front of the room? Have you lingered at the edge of some stylish circle trying to find your tongue while the truth was pilloried or a friend's good name was dragged through the dirt? Persuasion and peer pressure, whether on the playground, in the boardroom, or on the television, can cast a spell far more formidable than any witch's incantation.

This is why *resistance* has to be the believer's daily watchword. "Do not be conformed to this world," wrote Paul to a church situated at the heart of a culture every bit as high-pressured and subtly coercive as our own. Instead "be transformed by the renewing of your mind" (Romans 12:2). "Resist the devil," said James, "and he will flee from you" (James 4:7).

The marvelous thing is how quickly the enemy takes flight at the first sign of serious opposition. The illusions of the devil, like the enchantments of the Emerald Witch, have a way of vanishing the instant someone finds the courage to question their validity. If you doubt this, try putting *your* foot in the fire the next time the conjuror's sleep-inducing haze begins to fill the room. Speak up. Don't be afraid to go against the flow. Defy the persuader's assertions. Laugh out loud at the advertiser's claims. Toss the salesman's bill of goods out the window. Then watch as heads begin to turn, as eyes lose that glazed and distant look, as light dawns in one face and another there, and the dream cloud disperses like a puff of smoke in the wind.

But don't expect to get off easy. Jesus didn't. Neither did the prophets and the apostles. As Puddleglum found, it takes sweat, grit, and excruciating effort to meet this kind of challenge. Not only that, it can prove costly and painful. Putting your foot in the fire is likely to hurt. After all, the Witch, the devil, and their fellow hoax-mongers don't take kindly to people who make a habit of exposing their myths and shattering their deceptions. But then there's nothing like a little pain for putting the situation in perspective.

Puddleglum's hardheadedness is a quality no Christian can afford to be without. For when we make a decision to follow Jesus, we enter into a life-and-death struggle with evil, temptation, and deception, a struggle in which no one prevails except by stubborn resistance. Ultimate victory, of course, comes by the power of Christ alone. And yet the Master never shrinks from exhorting us to fight hard and hang tough, for only "he who endures to the end shall be saved" (Mark 13:13).

REFLECTION

Freedom is worth a few burnt toes.

BUNGLED BUT
BLESSED

✳

Jill, sitting astride the majestic Centaur's back, shivered in
the cold wind. Up above Cair Paravel's topmost tower the
golden banner bearing the great rampant lion fluttered and
snapped at half-staff. Down on the quay, through the swing-
ing shadows of the royal galleon's tall masts, four knights in
full armor were moving solemnly toward the castle, bearing
between them a body on a stately bier. Mournful music
floated over the heads of the gathered people. From this side
and that cries of "The king is dead; long live the king!"
drifted to her ears. Just in front of the ship she could see
Rilian, his hat in his hand and his chin on his breast, a small,
dark, helpless-looking figure beneath the bright, heraldic

127

shields that hung along the vessel's painted bulwarks. She had to bite her lip in order to keep back the tears.

What a sad and terrible day! And what a bitterly fitting ending to the botched and bungled series of adventures she'd had with Eustace and Puddleglum in the northern wastelands. To be sure, they'd made it back alive. And they *had* rescued the prince from the Emerald Witch's underground domain—but just barely in time for him to briefly embrace his father and receive his father's blessing before the aged king Caspian died. *It figures,* thought Jill.

That discouraging reflection set the wheels of her memory spinning painfully. Slowly at first, then with increasing rapidity, the details of her sojourn in the land of Narnia rose up and paraded themselves before her mind's eye, scene after excruciating scene.

She flinched and winced. Since the day of her arrival, it seemed, she hadn't been able to do a single thing right. She'd caused Eustace to fall off a cliff. She'd behaved very badly during her first meeting with Aslan. She'd muffed nearly all the "signs" the Lion had entrusted to her care. She'd missed the ruined giant city in the snowstorm—only when it was too late had she recognized the crucial message written in the stones of its foundation. Through her selfish wish for a hot bath and a good meal, she and her companions had almost ended up in a giant pie. Jill groaned. Why, oh why had Aslan brought her here in the first place?

"I wish I were at home," she moaned, slipping off her mount.

Eustace, sliding down beside her, merely shrugged and nodded in agreement. His face reflected the gloom of his mood.

"I have come."

Both children jumped at the unexpected rumble of a low thunderous voice speaking somewhere just behind them. They turned to see Aslan, his golden head bent low, his eyes glowing like two stars and fixed intently upon them. So real and solid was the Lion that everything around him seemed to fade into a mist.

Jill caught her breath. How could she face him? Again the procession of accusing memories began to march through her memory. She opened her mouth to say "I'm sorry." But the Lion, as if he could read her mind, stopped her short.

"Think of that no more," he said, caressing her cheek with his tongue. "You have done the work for which I sent you into Narnia."

*   *   *   *   *

At the center of the action of Leo Tolstoy's multiplotted, many-layered, thickly populated epic novel, *War and Peace*, stands the odd figure of Pierre Bezhukov, one of the quirkiest protagonists ever to grace the pages of a great work of fiction. Pierre, a young Russian nobleman with a French name, is a study in contradictions and contrasts, a man of widely varied and seemingly incompatible qualities. But of all his many memorable and distinguishing traits, perhaps the most important was this: Pierre was a confirmed bungler.

Though he usually meant well, Pierre made a mess of his life in almost every conceivable way. He lacked motivation. He was a disappointment to his dying father. Instead of entering a respectable career, he spent his time carousing and playing pranks on policemen. He married the wrong person for the wrong reasons. When Napoleon's armies invaded Russia, Pierre, though a civilian and a noncombatant, somehow managed to be taken as a prisoner of war. His life was one long string of tragicomic mistakes and miscalculations.

But that's not the end of the story. For in spite of this penchant for blundering, Pierre came to a happy ending. At the conclusion of the novel, the bungler was blessed. He regained his freedom, saw the French army routed, and married his true soul mate. Why? The answer, in a word, is *grace*. According to Tolstoy, life is more than the sum total of our personal triumphs and gaffes. There's always a wild card in the deck, the wild card of God's providence and loving care.[62]

Bungled but blessed. That, in a nutshell, is the theme of *The Silver Chair*. As viewed through the eyes of Jill Pole, this initially promising adventure rapidly degenerated into a fiasco every bit as botched as the life of Pierre Bezhukov. It's a tale of critical memory lapses, missed opportunities, fumbled signs, and miscalculations of character. But, as in Pierre's case, that's not the whole story. For just when Jill was convinced that her failure was complete, Aslan met her with surprising news. Blunders notwithstanding, he declared, her mission *had* been accomplished. Though bungled, Jill's adventure in the land of Narnia ended up blessed. How was this possible? Puddleglum knew the answer all along: "There *are* no accidents. Our guide is Aslan."

Fumbles and blunders, slipups and trip ups—most of us can't get through a single day without them. But when Christ is our guide, even our most glaring errors have an amazing way of fitting into the overall plan. God has promised us as much: "We know that all things work together for good to those who love God, to those who are the called according to His purpose" (Romans 8:28).

The man who penned those words wasn't simply indulging in a bit of wishful thinking. On the contrary, Paul had seen this principle played out in his own experience. In looking back over his life, he could discern how the wild card had been played. He was convinced that each and every one of his mistakes, both conscious and unconscious, had been used by God to promote His sovereign purposes. That's why, when on trial before the Jewish Sanhedrin, the apostle was able to make this shocking statement: "Men and brethren, I have lived in all good conscience before God until this day" (Acts 23:1).

Can these be the words of a man who, by his own admission, did "many things contrary to the name of Jesus of Nazareth" (Acts 26:9)? who "persecuted the church of God beyond measure and tried to destroy it" (Galatians 1:13)?

The answer, of course, is *yes*. Paul was able to make this assertion without flinching because he knew beyond a shadow of a doubt that the Lord had been his faithful guide every step of the way, even during his long dark years of self-willed blindness and pride. Paul believed that Christ had "separated [him] from [his] mother's womb and called [him] through His grace" (Galatians 1:15). In other words, his security rested on the knowledge that he *belonged* to God from first to last. And he was certain that, where the King of the universe is in control, there can be no accidents.

Are *you* a fumbler? Have you muffed the signs, misunderstood the directions, and made a hopeless mess of your life? If so, don't make the biggest mistake of all: Don't jump to conclusions before you get to the final chapter. As Paul put it, "Judge nothing before the time, until the Lord comes, who will both bring to light the hidden things of darkness and reveal the counsels of the hearts. Then each one's praise will come from God" (1 Corinthians 4:5).

Did you catch that? *Praise* is coming—to *you*. If your hope is fixed upon the Guide, it doesn't matter how badly you've bungled. In the end, you *will* be blessed.

REFLECTION
Where grace prevails, even mistakes can result
in something good.

"NARNIA AND THE NORTH!"

Unnhh! grunted Shasta, throwing both arms over the horse's broad dappled back and wildly kicking both legs in a blind attempt to find the stirrup with his left foot.

"Not like *that!*" grumbled the horse (a Talking Beast who called himself Bree). "You can't *climb* me as if I were a hill or a haystack!"

This was Shasta's second attempt at mounting. Setting out on adventures was proving to be more complicated than he'd expected; he hadn't realized that a horse's back stood quite so high off the ground. But though trembling with exertion and sweating profusely, he knew very well that he'd never been happier or more excited in his entire life. A talking horse! A chance to escape from the old fisherman! Best of all, a trip north! He pinched himself to make sure he wasn't dreaming.

"You might try putting your foot into the stirrup *first*," suggested Bree. "That's the idea. Now grip the pommel with both hands—good!—and then swing your other leg over. Ready? One . . . two . . . by the Lion! I believe you've done it!"

"I have!" agreed Shasta from the saddle. "I have indeed!" He had to clap one hand over his mouth to keep from shouting out loud in triumph. It wouldn't do to wake the two men inside the hut.

After a pause, he leaned forward and bent close to Bree's ear. "All my life," he whispered, "I've dreamed of the north. I used to sit out here mending the nets, staring up at that hill for hours on end, wondering what might lie beyond. Don't ask me why. I can't tell you. Somehow, *north* has always seemed to be where I belong."

"No need to ask," said the horse. "I can tell you why. You're a pure-blooded, freeborn northerner yourself. Nothing could be more obvious."

Shasta sat up and blinked. "You really think so?"

"I *know* so." The horse cocked an ear in the direction of the fisherman's squalid hut. "Surely you don't suppose that you were ever any son of *his?*"

"Well, I . . ."

136

"Not a chance!" snorted Bree. Then he arched his neck and stamped impatiently. "In any case," he said, "it's time we were off! Narnia and the North!"

Shasta felt the blood rush into his face. He sat a little straighter in the saddle. "*Narnia and the North!*" he responded enthusiastically.

The next moment they were flying up over the hill and down into the wide green plain beyond.

* * * * *

In the story of Shasta and his travels with a horse named Bree we return to a familiar theme, the theme of desire as a pivotal element in the dynamic spiritual life.

We've already met this idea in the history of Reepicheep, the indefatigable Mouse whose entire existence was organized around a single overpowering wish: to explore the ends of the earth and come at last to Aslan's country. Reepicheep knew exactly what he was after and pursued it relentlessly. He was the embodiment of the spirit that was at work in the apostle Paul when he wrote, "One thing I do . . . I press toward the goal" (Philippians 3:13-14).

Shasta, the young hero of *The Horse and His Boy*, was cut from another cloth. Most readers will probably identify with him far more readily than with the redoubtable, swashbuckling Mouse. For while Shasta, like Reepicheep, was motivated by desire, his was a desire of a very different kind. In part, it was nothing more than a vague sense of not belonging, of being a stranger in the only place he'd ever been able to call home. But it went far beyond this. For reasons he didn't comprehend and couldn't have explained, Shasta was consumed with a deep, almost inarticulate desire to go north.

"So is there in us a world of love to somewhat," wrote C. S. Lewis in *Surprised by Joy* (quoting seventeenth-century English poet Thomas Traherne), "though we know not what in the world it should be."[63] This is Shasta's story in a nutshell. He was a victim of what the Germans call *Sehnsucht*: an ardent yearning after a nameless, indefinable object. Lewis referred to it as a "lifelong nostalgia—" "our longing to be reunited with something in the universe from which we now feel cut off, to be on the inside of some door which we have always seen from the outside."[64]

It's significant that Lewis linked Shasta's *Sehnsucht* to the north. Here is a piece of imagery that came straight out of the author's personal experience. For "northernness," as George Sayer pointed out, "was one of the most important loves of [Jack's] life; it became a description of a particular imaginative world."[65]

Whence this fascination with northernness? It all began, Lewis said, with his adolescent enthusiasm for Norse mythology and a poignant line from Longfellow's poem "Tegner's Drapa": "I heard a voice that said, 'Balder the Beautiful is dead, is dead!'"

I knew nothing about Balder; but instantly I was up-
lifted into huge regions of northern sky, I desired with
almost sickening intensity something never to be described (except that it is cold, spacious, severe, pale,
and remote).[66]

"Desire . . . sickening intensity . . . something never to be
described." These are the defining characteristics of the "imaginative world" that, for young Jack Lewis, was summed up in
"the northernness." Over time his love for this world grew and
developed into a mythic symbol of his personal quest for spiritual fulfillment. In yearning for those "huge regions of northern
sky," Jack, like Shasta, was acknowledging his own incomplete-
ness. He was also bearing unwitting testimony to his birthright
as a child of God and his citizenship in a land beyond the narrow confines of existence in an English boarding school or an
industrial seaport town.

Have you ever felt that bittersweet pang, that stab of joy,
that soul-piercing arrow of heartbreaking loveliness and longing that, for Lewis and Shasta, was "shot from the North"?[67] It
comes to each of us in a different way. We encounter it in the
light of a red gold sunset, the melancholy of a misty seascape,
the cold gleam of stars among bare branches on a winter's
night; in "the smell of a bonfire, the sound of wild ducks flying overhead, the title of *The Well at the World's End*, the opening

lines of *Kubla Khan*, the morning cobwebs in late summer, or the noise of falling waves."[68] Wherever we meet it, it confronts us with inescapable evidence that we, like Jack and Shasta and the Old Testament patriarchs, are "strangers and pilgrims on the earth" (Hebrews 11:13), exiles in a foreign land, hoping to discover a way back home.

Put yourself in Shasta's place. You're sitting on the seashore, absently mending the nets, gazing off longingly toward the north. Do you sense the undertow of nagging restlessness? Can you relate to the undefined feelings of homesickness, the ache of unspoken discontent? If you can, you may begin to have some idea of what the Bible means when it says that God "has put eternity in [our] hearts" (Ecclesiastes 3:11).

The implications are well worth pondering.

REFLECTION

We were meant for bigger and better things.

MOST UNFORTUNATE

✳

Shasta had had a rough life. Abandoned as an infant, he was found floating in a boat by a fisherman who later pretended to be his father but used him as a servant. Shasta first realized that he was really an orphan when he overheard the fisherman trying to sell him to an even worse master. That is when he fled with a talking horse named Bree and headed north to seek freedom in the great land of Narnia.

Sitting alone, he reflected upon his misery. "I think I must be the most unfortunate boy that ever lived in the whole world. Everything goes right for everyone except me."

A pity party? Perhaps. But with good reason. After being frightened by a lion on their journey northward, Shasta and the noble warhorse encountered two other traveling companions heading to Narnia—a girl named Aravis and her mare named Hwin. Along the way, the four faced many dangers, including several fearsome lion encounters, one of which wounded the young girl. Eventually, Shasta was separated from the group and forced to press on alone. Now he sat—lost, cold, and hungry—weeping over his many misfortunes.

Suddenly, panic filled Shasta's heart as he heard loud breathing coming from the brush.

"What's that? Who's there? I know you're there somewhere. Who are you?" Shasta called to the darkness.

"One who has waited long for you to speak," came the majestic reply.

Unable to see anyone, wondering if he had encountered a mountain giant or ghoul, Shasta's wavering voice pleaded with the mysterious creature to go away and leave him alone. "I am the unluckiest person in the whole world."

But then Aslan, his breathing now a soothing sound to Shasta, invited the boy to share his sorrows.

"If only you knew what my life has been like," began Shasta. "I'm no better than an orphan. I've never known my real mother or father, and I was brought up by a cruel fisherman. And then finally, I was able to escape. But for what?" Shasta went on to describe his many trials.

"I do not call you unfortunate," Aslan interrupted.

"But what about all my trouble? If nothing else, it was bad luck to meet so many lions," argued Shasta.

"You met only one lion," Aslan corrected. "But he was swift of foot."

"How do you know?"

"I was the lion!" proclaimed Aslan, opening Shasta's frightened eyes to the real story behind his miserable tale. "I was the lion who forced you to join with Aravis. I was the cat who comforted you among the tombs. I was the lion who drove the jackals from you while you slept. I was the lion who gave the horses the new strength of fear for the last mile so that you should reach King Lune in time. And I was the lion you do not remember who pushed the boat in which you lay, a child near death, so that it came to shore where a man sat, wakeful at midnight, to receive you."

At that moment, Shasta's self-pity and fear dissolved into a mysterious recognition. Had it not been for the fisherman, he would not have fled to Narnia. Had he not fled, he would never have stumbled onto a conspiracy that revealed his place as future king. And had he not been chased by the lion, he would have quit too soon for success. As it turned out, the scenes of Shasta's story he would have preferred to avoid were the ones most important to the larger drama and to his own honored destiny.

* * * * *

It is the question never fully answered, yet continually asked: "Why do bad things happen to good people?" Or more precisely, "Why do bad things happen to me?"

The ensuing silence is deafening—and disturbing. We expect an explanation. No one likes to be kept in the dark. Every actor wants to know the full story. To be honest, we want a bit more than that. We want to direct the full story, dictating what scenes will and won't make it onto life's stage. The good things—adventure, romance, enjoyment—we'll keep. The bad—pain, sorrow, confusion—we won't. That's how it would be if we were in charge. But that's not how it is.

Still, there is good news. To repeat the words of Paul, already quoted in connection with Jill's blunders and mistakes:

We know that all things work together for good to those who love God, to those who are the called according to His purpose. For whom He foreknew, He also predestined to be conformed to the image of His Son.
(ROMANS 8:28-29)

Nothing, not even the painful times, will be wasted. It will all be redeemed and used for our good. But that is not necessarily the same thing as our happiness, our pleasure, our comfort, or even our protection. To be conformed is, by definition, a painful process. No artist ever formed clay into useful pottery without some pounding, squeezing, and eventual baking in the scorching oven.

There was a time in the life of C. S. Lewis when he would have changed the script if possible. His wife, the person he loved more than anyone else, was dying from a cruel form of cancer. He watched helplessly as life gradually and painfully drained from her body. Jack felt all of the emotions you might expect: anger, confusion, and—when it was over—intense grief. God had taken his bride, leaving an awful ache and a gaping whole in his heart.

Lewis, like Shasta, considered himself "most unfortunate" and expected an explanation that never came. The book *A Grief Observed* grew out of that torturous journey—his journal through the darkest days of agony, including sometimes scandalous honesty about what we feel when going through the unpleasant scenes of life's story.

"What do people mean when they say, 'I am not afraid of God because I know He is good'?" Lewis asked while he struggled to reconcile a good God with a bad life. "Have they never even been to a dentist?" Sometimes, he concluded, the pain we'd like to avoid is necessary for our ultimate good.

> The terrible thing is that a perfectly good God is in this matter hardly less formidable than a Cosmic Sadist. The more we believe that God hurts only to heal, the less we can believe that there is any use in begging for tenderness. . . . Suppose that what you are up against is a surgeon whose intentions are wholly good. The kinder and more conscientious he is, the more inexorably he will go on cutting.[69]

God is good. And that is the problem. He weaves all things toward eventual redemption, including the scenes we would rather avoid. He never promised to spare us from hurt or lead us beyond the valley of the shadow of death. That would ruin the story being told and make our lives truly "most unfortunate."

Someday, like Shasta, we will meet the great King and Author of history. Only then will our eyes be opened to the moments in which He was "the Lion" orchestrating events toward a greater purpose—a greater good. Only then will we better understand how and when the grand drama of providence intersected the smaller scenes of our lives.

In him we were chosen, having been predestined according to the plan of him who works out everything in conformity with the purpose of his will, in order that we, who were the first to hope in Christ, might be for the praise of his glory. (EPHESIANS 1:11-12, NIV)

REFLECTION
The scenes we least like may be most crucial
to the story being told.

"But think of the good we could do!"
said Shift. . . . "And everyone would
have to obey us, even the King himself.
We would set everything right in Narnia."

—*THE LAST BATTLE*, CHAPTER 1, "BY CALDRON POOL"

THE GOOD WE COULD DO

❋

"Now just stand still and stop your fidgeting," said the ape irritably. "How do you expect me to get you properly fitted and hitched up?"

Poor Puzzle, the old gray donkey, squeezed his eyes shut and ground his teeth. He couldn't help shuddering as his companion dragged the heavy lion skin up over his head and down along his back. Already he felt hot, prickly, and uncomfortable under the big yellow pelt. A dreadful trembling seized him, spreading from his nostrils to his ears and then down the length of his body until it set his tail to twitching.

"Are you sure this is a good idea, Shift?" he said.

Shift snorted as he shoved the lion head back over Puzzle's

nose. "As if *you'd* recognize a good idea if it hit you between the eyes! Haven't I told you a million times to leave the thinking to me?"

"*Ee-aw!*" moaned Puzzle. "I know you're far cleverer than I am, being so much like a man and all. But I still can't help feeling that there's something *improper* about an old donkey like me going about dressed up as . . . *ow!*"

"How you *do* talk!" grunted Shift, cinching up the girth strings under Puzzle's belly with a hard yank. "Why, anyone would think you fancied yourself an intelligent creature! I've thought the whole thing out, I tell you. You don't suppose it was by mere accident that this skin came tumbling down the waterfall to us?"

"Well . . ."

"Don't you know there's a purpose in everything? It all works out for the best. Now hush up and let me have a look at you."

The ape shambled a few steps away, turned, and studied his handiwork judiciously. Slowly, a wicked grin spread over his face. "It's perfect!" he said at last. "Why, if anyone saw you now, they'd think you were Aslan himself!"

"But I don't want them to think that!" brayed the donkey.

"It's not a question of what you want," said the ape. "It's about what's best for Narnia. Don't you see what a great responsibility you've taken on?"

"But—"

"Stop blubbering. Can't you understand that we're just *borrowing* a bit of the Great Lion's authority? *Appropriating* some of his power in a beneficent cause? They'll *have* to listen to us now! Just think of the good we'll be able to accomplish!"

"But what would *he* say?"

At that moment a clap of thunder split the sky above and shook the earth beneath. The ape and the donkey were thrown to the ground. Poor Puzzle cowered under the lionskin and groaned.

* * * * *

We live in the age of "can do"—an era in which the impossibilities of the past have become the commonplaces of the present. Cure tuberculosis? Can do. Send men and women into space? Can do. Transplant vital organs? Genetically engineer superior soybeans? Clone a sheep? Can do. Clone a human being?

What we *should* do is ask another question, a question fewer and fewer people bother to ask.

Shift, the sinister simian who precipitated the apocalyptic events of *The Last Battle,* hadn't the slightest interest in such questions. He was an ape, not a man, but manlike enough to recognize opportunity when it came knocking. Shift possessed the skill to take an old lionskin and turn it into a mantle of power. He had the vision to use that power to reshape the world according to his own specifications. Puzzle the donkey,

Shift's simpleminded sidekick, may have had misgivings about
the idea. But the ape knew how to counter his objections: "Just
think of the good we could do!"

There were only two problems with Shift's plan. In the
first place, the "good" he claimed to be doing wasn't good
at all. It was "good" only in the sense that it promoted his
personal interests; it was grasping and greedy and self-
aggrandizing. In the second place, even if his aims had been
noble, his methods were all wrong. For as Shift was to discover the hard way, it is impossible to achieve good ends by
evil means.

Perhaps we can forgive the ape for failing to see this from
the beginning. His lack of perception was, after all, primarily
a matter of his innate temperament and characteristic outlook on life. To put it bluntly, Shift was a "can do" kind of
creature. He was a pragmatist, a practical-minded utilitarian.
It was a trait he shared with most of Narnia's archvillains.

Take the witches for example—White, Emerald, or any
other color you like. Most witches, explained Lewis in *The
Magician's Nephew,* "are not interested in things or people unless they can use them; they are terribly practical."[70] Young
Digory's despicable uncle Andrew was of a similar bent: He
"thinks he can do anything he likes to get anything he
wants."[71] Then there's Nikabrik, the hotheaded dwarf who
hoped to defeat King Miraz by calling up the White Witch
from the dead. "There's power, if you like," he said in de-

fense of his dreadful proposal. "There's something practical."[72]

Practical power. Power to get things done. That's what Shift was after. That's why he never bothered to ask himself whether he really ought to fool the rest of the world by passing off a silly donkey as the king of all beasts. His blindness to the truth illustrates an important principle: A "can do" mentality may be fine as far as it goes, but it can't help us decide what we *should* do. For that we require a different frame of reference.

This last thought contains a clue to the deeper reason for Shift's eventual demise. The ape wasn't merely pragmatic. He was irreverent. He had no regard for the transcendent truths and realities that might have kept him from folly and protected him against self-destruction. The real Aslan meant nothing to him except as a pawn in the game of self-advancement. If Aslan could be harnessed to the cart of Shift's master plan, well and good. If not, then Aslan's nemesis, the Calormene god, Tash, would do. God and the devil, heaven and hell, angels, demons, and immortal souls—all, as far as Shift was concerned, were to be valued simply as means to his predetermined ends.

This is the mind-set that Christ rejected with the words, "You shall not tempt the Lord your God" (Matthew 4:7; Deuteronomy 6:16). He saw very clearly that His Father is not willing to become a mere adjunct to human schemes and dreams. He is not necessarily waiting in the wings to catch us whenever we choose to take a mad leap—not for all "the good we could do" by means of such an attention-getting feat. Jesus understood that "practical power" of this sort has no place in the divine economy.

Again, the devil took Him up on an exceedingly high mountain, and showed Him all the kingdoms of the world and their glory. And he said to Him, "All these things I will give You if You will fall down and worship me." Then Jesus said to him, "Away with you, Satan! For it is written, You shall worship the Lord your God, and Him only you shall serve.'" (MATTHEW 4:8-10)

Unlike Shift, Jesus knew when to let opportunity pass Him by. He renounced pragmatism, refused to use God's power for His own purposes, and chose to worship instead. Ultimately, it was reverence that enabled Him to understand what He *should* and *should not* do. His eyes were fixed on a higher standard than that of practical utilitarianism.

"There is a way that seems right to a man," said Solomon, "but its end is the way of death" (Proverbs 14:12).

And the way of death is the way of death—in spite of "the good we could do."

REFLECTION
What seems right may be wrong.

SEEING IT

✳

The war was finally over, the battle for Narnia lost. Tirian and
his friends had put up a valiant fight. But the foe was too
mighty for such a tiny company, even with help from Eustace
and Jill, the friends of Narnia from another world. They now
found themselves in a new place. Well, not exactly a new
place—more like the real place of which old Narnia was a
mere shadow. It was like waking up in a world of bright,
warm, inviting color after a long journey through bleak, frigid,
crude grayness. It was lovely beyond description.

And then came a very strange and wonderful surprise.
Tirian, Eustace, and Jill met other friends of Narnia who'd

already arrived—Lucy, Edmund, and High King Peter, as well as Digory and Polly, the original visitors from another world. Each recounted the story of how he or she came to this mysterious place, including the awful moments leading up to Tirian's defeat when he and the children were thrown through what they presumed was death's door. As it turned out, the stable door was for them an entrance into unimaginable beauty and joy.

They quickly discovered that a group of Dwarfs had been flung through the door just ahead of Jill. But rather than explore and enjoy the wonders around them, the Dwarfs were doing something odd. All of them were just sitting closely together in a little circle facing one another. Lucy had attempted to make friends with them, but to no avail. So, at her request, Tirian decided to try.

"Look out!" a Dwarf named Diggle hollered as Tirian and the others approached. "Mind where you're going. Don't walk into our faces!" A strange reaction, since there was plenty of light to see them clearly. Eustace, who had no affection for the Dwarfs after the horrid ways they behaved during the battle for Narnia, reacted: "We're not blind. We've got eyes in our heads."

"They must be darn good ones if you can see in here," said Diggle. "In this pitch-black, poky, smelly little hole of a stable."

But they weren't sitting in a stable. They were surrounded

by the same inviting spectacle as the rest. Only they didn't see it. Or wouldn't see it.

"Can't you see?" asked Lucy. "Look up! Look round! Can't you see the sky and the trees and the flowers? Can't you see *me?*"

"How in the name of all Humbug can I see what ain't there? And how can I see you any more than you can see me in this pitch-darkness?"

It got quickly worse. Not only were the Dwarfs unable to see the bright beauty around them, they couldn't enjoy the lovely aromas filling the air. To their spoiled senses, even freshly picked flowers reeked of filthy stable-litter. Everything that was light, goodness, and beauty to the children seemed dark and wretched ugliness to the Dwarfs.

Not that Eustace or Jill should have been surprised. After all, these were the same Dwarfs who had blinded themselves to goodness in old Narnia. When Tirian and his comrades fought to defend justice and honor, the Dwarfs had refused to join. They had never actually sided with Shift the Ape or his wicked league, but neither would they help those on the side of good. Worse, they actually had hindered the noble effort by shooting arrows into Tirian's horses.

"The Dwarfs are for the Dwarfs!" they had taunted. "We don't want you to win any more than the other gang. You can't take *us* in."

Confronted with two possible choices, the Dwarfs had

opted out. They wanted neither the illicit servants of Tash nor the true servants of Aslan ruling their lives. They simply wanted to be left alone. Left to rule themselves. Left to see, or not see, as they wished.

And now they sat hunched together on the other side of death's door in the middle of bright, lovely goodness. But they couldn't, or rather they wouldn't, see a thing.

* * * * *

"If only God would show Himself," we ponder, "maybe they would believe."

It is a well-meaning wish. Those who have responded to God's good gifts want others to do the same. We want them to know joy rather than misery, color rather than grayness, sun rather than shadow. And so we hope God will do something dramatic to make Himself known.

But we are mistaken. God has already revealed Himself and shone His light for everyone to see.

What may be known of God is manifest in them, for God has shown it to them. For since the creation of the world His invisible attributes are clearly seen, being understood by the things that are made, even His eternal power and Godhead, so that they are without excuse, because, although they knew God, they did not glorify Him as God, nor were thankful, but became futile in their thoughts, and their foolish hearts were darkened. (ROMANS 1:19-21)

Certainly, not all have been given the same amount of light. But they have enough to move toward rather than away from its warm, inviting glow. Yet, even those standing closest to the Light's source can blind themselves to its radiance.

In Him was life, and the life was the light of men. And the light shines in the darkness, and the darkness did not comprehend it. That was the true Light, which gives light to every man coming into the world. He was in the world, and the world was made through Him, and the world did not know Him. (JOHN 1:4, 9-10)

"You can't take us in!" That was the Dwarfs' response to the light they were given. Rather than risk choosing wrongly, they made no choice at all. But no choice, as Jesus explained, is still a decision.

He who does not believe is condemned already, because he has not believed in the name of the only begotten Son of God. And this is the condemnation, that the light has come into the world, and men loved darkness rather than light. (JOHN 3:18-19)

Even when light glows faintly, it shows us the direction in which to move. The alternative to risk is not safety. It is the certain peril of stumbling around in pitch-blackness or the dismal paralysis of fearful distrust, the fear of making any move at all lest you be taken in to something you'd rather not.

C. S. Lewis could relate to the paralysis of indecision. He too worried that he might be "taken in" by faith, lured into believing something that might turn out to be mere fable or wishful thinking. That is why it took him so long to move toward the light of Christ. It is also why he placed the pathetically indecisive Dwarfs in his final story. Their pitiful fate represents what might have been his own.

Is it possible that the distant light is an oncoming train that will bring ruin? Perhaps. But it is more likely the promised light of God. Besides, what is there to lose? It is not as if sitting in the dark, smelly stable of unbelief is an existence worth preserving.

REFLECTION

God showing does not guarantee our seeing.

"I have come home at last! This is my real country! I belong here."

—*THE LAST BATTLE*, CHAPTER 15, "FURTHER UP AND FURTHER IN"

FURTHER UP AND FURTHER IN

✳

The excitement was almost too much to bear. "Don't stop! Further up and further in!" Farsight the Eagle called to the others as he flew upward, deeper into the wonders yet ahead.

Lucy, Edmund, Peter, Eustace, Jill, and the others were seeing and doing things they had never imagined possible, a deep longing mixed with the thrill of discovery pulling them all in the same direction. It was a risk-filled adventure, but without fear. They ran faster and faster, across valleys and over hills, every step increasing the anticipation that was never disappointed.

"Further up and further in!" another cried.

They saw the Unicorn swimming through the waterfall.

But he didn't swim down. He swam up—his long, white horn splitting the falling stream above. The children followed, somehow able to move against the thundering flow. Nothing like this was possible in the old world.

"Further up and further in!" Were the words spoken? Or were their hearts shouting from within?

They reached a golden gate that suggested the beginning of an even greater discovery. All stood silent, hesitant to approach. And then a wonderful thing happened. Out walked one who, to many, was an old friend. Red feather on his head and tiny sword by his side, the talking mouse bowed and said, "Welcome, in the Lion's name." It was none other than Reepicheep, the legendary Narnian hero and most noble and loyal companion to King Caspian the Seafarer. "Come further up and further in."

It was only the first of many reunions. Tirian felt his long deceased father's warm embrace. The children met all of their old Narnian friends—Fledge the winged horse who had carried Digory and Polly on their journey to retrieve the silver apple; Puddleglum the Marsh-wiggle who had helped Jill and Eustace free King Rilian from the green lady's evil enchantment; Trumpkin the Dwarf; the two good Beavers; and many others.

One of the best moments for Lucy was greeting her dear friend, Tumnus the Faun, who protected her from the White Witch to his own demise. The two walked and talked together, Tumnus helping Lucy understand more of this strange, wonderful place she was just beginning to love. She had noticed that the beauty and majesty increased as they journeyed.

"Of course, Daughter of Eve," said the Faun. "The further up and the further in you go, the bigger everything gets." This is the real Narnia, of which the old was a mere shadow. That was why everything seemed so familiar, but better. Like an onion—explained Tumnus—"except that as you continue to go in and in, each circle is larger than the last."

The Unicorn's words suddenly made more sense. "I have come home at last!" he had proclaimed upon reaching the outer ring of this place. "This is my real country! I belong here." It was the land he had been looking for without knowing it. The reason he and the others loved parts of old Narnia was because it looked a little like this, the real place.

If there was any doubt that they had reached home, it was dispelled when the great Lion himself, Aslan, appeared. Lucy and the others had arrived at the outskirts of his country, the place where death—as they referred to it in the Shadow-Lands—had no more power. "The holidays have begun," declared the Lion. "The dream is ended: this is the morning."

"Further up and further in."

It was like the opening pages of a wonderful storybook—"which goes on for ever: in which every chapter is better than the one before."

* * * * *

Imagine some of these delightful sensations: the rush of exhilaration as you run toward the most beautiful, inviting place you've ever seen; feeling a lump of joy in your throat as you are reunited with dearly loved friends and family after a long separation; digging in to second and third helpings of the most deliciously rich meal you've ever eaten at the end of a long fast—without a single worry about gaining weight or clogging arteries; allowing the warm breeze and crashing sounds of an ocean beach to refresh your spirit as you take time to watch the sun set and then rise on the horizon; knowing that every day will be more thrilling, relaxing, delicious, and joyous than the one before.

These are some of the images that fit C. S. Lewis's concept of heaven, our true home. They are very unlike those typically imagined by churchgoing folks—such as wearing an uncomfortable robe while sitting on an isolated cloud playing a harp, bored to tears but thankful because it is better than suffering in the other place. For Lewis, heaven was the ultimate and lasting realization of that which he had spent a lifetime craving but never having—the real thing of which earthly pleasures are a mere hint or taste. "Most people," he explained, "if they had really learned to look into their own hearts, would know that they do want, and want acutely, something that cannot be had in this world. There are all sorts of things in this world that offer to give it to you, but they never quite keep their promise."[73]

This process of desiring and tasting without satisfaction could drive us to despair. But it drove Lewis to hope because, in his words:

> If I find in myself a desire which no experience in this world can satisfy, the most probable explanation is that I was made for another world. If none of my earthly pleasures satisfy it, that does not prove that the universe is a fraud. Probably earthly pleasures were never meant to satisfy it, but only to arouse it, to suggest the real thing. . . . I must keep alive in myself the desire for my true country, which I shall not find till after death.[74]

It is that other world that Lucy, Peter, Edmund, and the other children finally experience at the culmination of the Narnia chronicles. Desire is fulfilled; tasting becomes feasting; anticipation turns to realization, longing to enjoying. As it turns out, the Unicorn was right. "The reason why we loved the old Narnia is that it sometimes looked a little like this."[75]

Jesus described our ultimate destination as a specially prepared part of his own house. "In My Father's house are many mansions. . . . I go to prepare a place for you" (John 14:2). He painted a verbal picture of a place where we would be rewarded and fulfilled. "His lord said to him, 'Well done, good and faithful servant; you were faithful over a few things, I will make you ruler over many things. Enter into the joy of your lord'" (Matthew 25:21). And He gave the apostle John a glimpse of the unspeakable joy we can expect when God and man finally experience the same reality and share the same home.

I saw a new heaven and a new earth, for the first heaven and the first earth had passed away. . . . And I heard a loud voice from heaven saying, "Behold, the tabernacle of God is with men, and He will dwell with them, and they shall be His people. God Himself will be with them and be their God. And God will wipe away every tear from their eyes; there shall be no more death, nor sorrow, nor crying. There shall be no more pain, for the former things have passed away."

(REVELATION 21:1, 3-4)

Heaven is not some stiff, happiness-deprived place. It is the place for which the deepest part of us feels homesick, complete with the sights, sounds, and smells we miss. There will probably be fresh cookies from the oven and lots of laughter around the table. Boredom will be impossible, because the adventure never ends and the story gets better with the turning of every page.

Heaven is where those who serve the great Lion on this side of death's door will find His welcome on the other. There will be a magnificent reception into the joy we've

craved as we are greeted with a smile, a hug, and an enthusiastic "Welcome home!"

> *I've a home beyond the river, I've a mansion bright and fair;*
> *I've a home beyond the river, I will dwell with Jesus there.*[76]

REFLECTION

Home is better than we can possibly imagine.

Afterthoughts

Our journey into the land of Narnia began in the quaint English pub Eagle and Child where, more than half a century ago, a group of staid Oxford dons gathered to discuss classic English literature over stout English ale and plain English pub food. It was as unlikely a place as any, perhaps, to discover a door into another world.

My hometown—Colorado Springs—has a pub of its own: Jack Quinn's Irish Alehouse. It's here that I propose to bring our tour of Narnia to a close. My selection of a landing place isn't as arbitrary as it might seem; from a certain perspective, a booth at Quinn's is the ideal spot to stop and reflect upon our trip to the land inside the wardrobe. For the entrance to Quinn's is itself a kind of a door into another world.

South Tejon Street is the hub of the Springs' modest nightlife: three or four blocks of trendy restaurants, chic shops, an "artsy" movie theatre, a dance club, a jazz and rock club, and, of course, the inevitable Starbucks (or two). In the middle of all this modernity sits Jack Quinn's, its gold-lettered, black and forest green facade reminiscent of some corner of James Joyce's Dublin. The pub's interior is literally a piece of old Ireland itself: The two long, polished bars, the ubiquitous dark oak paneling, and the high-backed booths are all said to have come straight out of a nineteenth-century Irish public house. Apparently it was all dismantled there, shipped across the Atlantic, and reassembled, London Bridge–like, here. The result? Quinn's has atmosphere—an ambience you won't find anywhere else in town (except, perhaps, at the Golden Bee, a pub at our town's famous resort, the Broadmoor).

It's my theory that atmosphere is the primary reason people patronize Quinn's. Food and Guinness can be had elsewhere. Not so the feeling of leaving El Paso County and stepping into County Kerry that you get as you cross the threshold at Quinn's. There's live music at Quinn's, too, traditional Irish music (the kind you used to hear in Irish pubs before the Irish caught on to country-western and karaoke). At least there was on the night I have in mind.

I was playing guitar in the band that evening. So was Tom, a cittern player who loves myth and fantasy as much as I do. Tom is an avid reader of Tolkien and MacDonald, E. R. Eddison and Peter Beagle, William Morris and C. S. Lewis. So it was only natural that when the band took a break, Tom and I, like those Oxford dons at the Eagle and Child, filled up the idle time with literary talk. The topic? Lord Dunsany's classic, *The King of Elfland's Daughter*—a sad, strange, unearthly tale about Alveric, a lovelorn prince who spent ten fruitless years listening for the horns of Elfland, seeking that country's elusive and ever retreating borders, searching desperately for his long-lost elfin bride.

"What I like about Dunsany," said Tom, "isn't so much the *story* he tells. It's the *atmosphere* he creates. It's that indefinable feeling of enchantment that comes over you when you're on the inside of one of his books, that sense of being transported to another place, another time, another world."

I glanced around the room and nodded. I knew exactly what he meant.

A New Region

I knew what Tom meant because I had felt the same thing myself many times. In fact, the more I thought about it, the more I realized that my friend had just summed up my whole reason for reading stories like *The King of Elfland's Daughter*. Since childhood, I've turned to books mainly as a means of transport, a way of getting beyond the gray wall of everyday life and out into some other place—a place of beauty and wonder and enchantment, a place with atmosphere.

That place has always been far more important to me than the events that transpire there. Just *being* in the world of the story—Mark Twain's Hannibal, James Herriot's Yorkshire, A. A. Milne's Hundred Acre Wood—*that*, to me, is the main thing. To put it another way, I prize setting above plot. This is why I've never had much sympathy with the contemporary impulse to "update" old stories: to rework *Romeo and Juliet* against the backdrop of New York City's gang culture, for instance, or turn the tale of Lancelot and Guinevere into a high school romance. Personally, I've had enough of modern cities and suburban high schools. What *I* want is Verona and Camelot. I'm seeking passage to Prydain, Sherwood Forest, Neverland, the Shire. In the words of William Morris, I'm irked with "the dullness of our town, and the littleness of men's doings therein."[77] I long to be touched by the light and breathe the air of a land outside the boundaries of my own pale and paltry experience.

Apparently I'm not alone. C. S. Lewis's own love for books had a similar origin and motivation. The pleasure he derived from his boyhood reading was largely a matter of savoring the peculiar ambience of a story's imagined world. Exciting narration, unexpected plot twists, clever characterizations—all of this was, for him, purely secondary. It wasn't the "Redskin dangers" of the Mohican woodlands that captured Lewis's imagination. Instead, "The 'Redskinnery' was what really mattered."[78]

This, it seems, is why he found George MacDonald's *Phantastes* so thoroughly captivating. According to his own testimony, what struck Jack most forcibly about this book was its unique atmosphere—"the air of the new region" that he discovered within its pages.[79] "I did not yet know (and I was long in learning) the name of the new quality, the bright shadow, that rested on the travels of Anodos. I do now. It was Holiness," he said.[80]

It is impossible to overstate the importance of that "quality." As he stepped beneath the eaves of MacDonald's enchanted forest, something came over Lewis that literally changed his life. Under the influence of that "bright shadow," he began moving down a path that eventually led him to become one of history's greatest Christian thinkers and apologists. From that point forward, the air of the new region was to inspire and inform everything he did.

Taking Us There

This is especially true of his work as an author. If Jack's reading habits were driven by this hunger for atmosphere and ambience, we can be certain that a great deal of his writing was fueled by the same impulse. One might even go so far as to say that it represents the very heart of his storytelling—at least where Narnia is concerned.

We already know that *The Chronicles of Narnia* were not born of careful plotting or clever allegorizing. Lewis said, "Everything began with images; a faun carrying an umbrella, a queen on a sledge, a magnificent lion."[81] But what was the point of the imagery? What, if anything, did he hope to accomplish by presenting pictures of fauns, witches, and lions to his readers' imagination? A comment of George Sayer's may be helpful at this point:

> Jack's main object was, of course, to write good sto-
> ries. He was also concerned with the atmosphere of
> separate adventures and incidents and with fidelity to
> the complex world of his imagination.[82]

Atmosphere. The complex world of his imagination. These, along with effective narrative drama, seem to be what Lewis had in view when he began dreaming of centaurs and Talking Beasts, of Lantern Waste and Dancing Lawn. In other words, the imagery of Narnia was not invented for its own sake. It exists to serve a higher purpose. Every bit of it, from the White Witch's endless winter to the rich aroma of Aslan's fur to the heraldic banners snapping in the breeze above Cair Paravel's towers, is calculated to cultivate atmosphere—to foster a certain mood and create a certain sense of place.

Here's my point: As I see it, the really vital thing about the Narnia stories is Narnia itself. What I love best about these seven books is the place that comes to life between their fourteen covers. Like Quinn's, it's a place with atmosphere, a carefully conceived and painstakingly constructed atmosphere. Even better, it's a place where readers can breathe the "air of a new region" and come under the influence of a "bright shadow," the same "bright shadow" that Lewis encountered in the land of *Phantastes.*

I can't help feeling that this is exactly what Jack intended when he sat down to pen these remarkable tales. Having been to Fairyland himself, he was compelled to return and take the rest of us with him. To be sure, *The Chronicles of Narnia* contain some of the most masterful storytelling in all English literature. And yes, they are packed from beginning to end with lots of profound and practical theology. But the thing they do best, in my humble opinion, is the same thing that Lord Dunsany does for Tom and that Jack Quinn's does for its patrons: They lift us out of our drab, everyday existence and transport us to another world.

Never a Possession

Late that night at Quinn's the lights were low. The band was finishing its last set of the night. Between numbers I could hear the light laughter of a few diehard patrons as it rose from a corner booth and floated across the room in a swirl of tobacco smoke. I checked my tuning and watched the bartender draw a pint of dark ale from the tap. Then the fiddler touched bow to string and we were off into a set of jigs: "The Rambling Pitchfork," "The Tenpenny Bit," "The Rose in the Heather."

As the music built and swelled, Tom's words came drifting back to me: "Another place, another time, another world." I turned them over in my mind and smiled. Why put an Irish pub in the middle of Colorado Springs? Why bother playing obscure Celtic folk tunes in the era of rock and rap? Why waste time dreaming of dwarfs and fauns at the height of the Oxford academic term? The answer isn't far to seek. It's a question of breathing the air of another world—dim and close and smoky though it may be.

I struck the final chord of the last tune. The wail of the pipes faded and died away. We stowed the sound equipment and packed up our gear. Hefting my guitar case, I recrossed the threshold and stepped out into the glare of the downtown night. The next day I would be back in the office, back in the sterile land of cubicles and computers and corporate dress codes. But right then I had time to take one last look at that forest green facade and that gold-lettered sign—Jack Quinn's Irish Alehouse and Pub. I savored the last few moments of my temporary sojourn in another world.

It's always temporary, of course. C. S. Lewis knew this. He understood that while we live in the flesh, our opportunities to breathe the air of the world beyond the wardrobe will be fleeting and few and brief. Even our best storytellers and mythmakers—those who are most skilled at getting us over the wall—rarely manage to take us all the way to the fabled Isle of the Hesperides; as Lewis put it, the net they weave "very seldom does succeed in catching the bird."[83] Even when they do succeed, as I believe Lewis does supremely in *The Chronicles of Narnia*, the atmosphere they create fades all too quickly. It's never long before reality sets in and we find ourselves, like Lord Dunsany's Alveric, reaching for something that is always receding just beyond our grasp.

That's when it's helpful to remember that we were not made for this world, and that for this very reason our greatest joy "is never a possession, always a desire for something longer ago or further away or still 'about to be.' "[84] That's when we begin to understand what Lewis meant when he said that the heart of reality is not, after all, a place, but a Person.[85] That's when we need to ponder anew the well-worn words of Augustine: "You have made us for Yourself, and our hearts are restless until they can find peace in You."[86]

"No wonder," wrote George Sayer, "that my little stepdaughter, after she had read all the Narnia stories, cried bitterly, saying, 'I don't want to go on living in this world. I want to live in Narnia with Aslan.'"

No wonder indeed. And no wonder Sayer answered: "Darling, one day you will."[87]

Jim Ware

Endnotes

1. Downing, David, *The Most Reluctant Convert: C. S. Lewis's Journey to Faith* (Downers Grove, Ill.: InterVarsity Press, 2002), 11.

2. Ibid.

3. Ibid., 66.

4. C. S. Lewis, "Sometimes Fairy Stories May Say Best What's to Be Said," in *Of Other Worlds* (San Diego: Harcourt Brace Jovanovich, 1966), 36.

5. Lyle W. Dorsett and Marjorie Lamp Mead, eds., *C. S. Lewis: Letters to Children* (New York: Scribner, 1996).

6. C. S. Lewis, *The Voyage of the "Dawn Treader"* (New York: Collier Books, 1952), 246–247.

7. Dorsett and Mead, *Letters to Children.*

8. C. S. Lewis, *The Magician's Nephew* (New York: Collier Books, 1955), 148.

9. C. S. Lewis, *Mere Christianity* (New York: Collier Books, 1952), 51.

10. C. S. Lewis, *The Great Divorce* (New York: Simon & Schuster, 1996), 74.

11. C. S. Lewis, *Prince Caspian* (New York: Collier Books, 1951), 211.

12. From *Cover Stories*, BBC Radio.

13. Francis Thompson, "The Kingdom of God: 'In No Strange Land,'" in *The Complete Poetical Works of Francis Thompson* (New York: Boni and Liveright, Inc., 1913).

14. *Cover Stories* (emphasis added).

15. Ibid.

16. Rudolf Otto, *The Idea of the Holy* (Oxford, England: Oxford University Press, 1923).

17. John Calvin, *The Best of John Calvin* (Grand Rapids, Mich.: Baker Book House, 1981), 202, 211.

18. Christina Rosetti, "Mid-Winter," in *Behold That Star: A Christmas Anthology* (Rifton, New York: Plough Publishing House, 1966).

19. Gandalf the Grey, the Hobbits' wizard-guide in J. R. R. Tolkien's *The Lord of the Rings*, falls into darkness in the mines of Moria and subsequently returns as Gandalf the White.

20. Hilaire Belloc, quoted in G. K. Chesterton, *Orthodoxy* (New York: Image Books, 1959).

21. On this concept of sub-creation, see J. R. R. Tolkien, "On Fairy-Stories," in *The Tolkien Reader* (New York: Ballantine Books, 1966), 46.

22. G. K. Chesterton, *The Everlasting Man* (New York: Image Books, 1955), 36.

23. Alexander Pope, "An Essay on Man," in *The Complete Poetical Works of Alexander Pope* (London: Macmillan and Company, 1885), 201.

24. Plato, *Phaedrus*, in *Great Books of the Western World*, vol. 7 (Chicago: Encyclopedia Britannica, Inc., 1952), 116.

25. C. S. Lewis, *The Weight of Glory* (Grand Rapids, Mich.: William B. Eerdmans, 1972), 14–15.

26. See also endnote 21. In his essay "On Fairy-Stories," J. R. R. Tolkien suggests that through art, story making, and other imaginative activities, human beings participate in the embellishment (or what he calls the "effoliation") of creation, thus reflecting their nature as creatures made in the image of God. For an elaboration of this idea in parable form, see his story "Leaf by

Niggle" in *The Tolkien Reader* (New York: Ballantine Books, 1966), 85–112.

27. George Sayer, *Jack: A Life of C. S. Lewis* (Wheaton, Ill.: Crossway Books, 1988), 315; Brian Sibley and Alison Sage, *A Treasury of Narnia* (London: HarperCollins, 1999), 58.

28. Focus on the Family Radio Theatre, introduction to *The Chronicles of Narnia: Prince Caspian,* adapted by Paul McCusker, 2003. See also Sayer, 315.

29. Lewis, *Mere Christianity*, 51.

30. Ibid.

31. Lewis, *Prince Caspian*, 142.

32. Fyodor Dostoevsky, *The Brothers Karamazov* (Chicago: Encyclopedia Britannica, Inc., 1952), 27.

33. C. S. Lewis, *Surprised by Joy* (Glasgow: William Collins Sons & Company, 1955), 172.

34. Sydney Carter, "The Lord of the Dance," copyright 1963 by Stainer & Bell Ltd., London.

35. C. S. Lewis, *Perelandra* (New York: Macmillan, 1944), 217.

36. Lewis, *Surprised by Joy,* 160.

37. C. S. Lewis, *Miracles* (New York: Macmillan, 1960), 136.

38. Dostoevsky, *The Brothers Karamazov,* 27.

39. "My Hope Is Built On Nothing Less," words by Edward Mote, music by William R. Bradbury.

40. *Out of the Silent Planet, Perelandra,* and *That Hideous Strength.*

41. C. S. Lewis, *The Pilgrim's Regress* (Grand Rapids, Mich.: William B. Eerdmans, 1958).

42. J. R. R Tolkien, *The Lord of the Rings* (Boston: Houghton Mifflin Company, 1955), from the dust jacket.

43. Herman Melville, footnote 2 in *Moby Dick* (New York: Macmillan, 1962), 200.

44. Samuel Taylor Coleridge, "The Rime of the Ancient Mariner," in *Samuel Taylor Coleridge: Selected Poems* (New York: Gramercy Books, 1996), 125.

45. Ibid., 137.

46. Ibid., 128.

47. Paraphrased from Matthew 26:26-28; Mark 14:22-25; Luke 22:19, 20; and I Corinthians 11:23-26.

48. C. S. Lewis, *Letters to Malcolm: Chiefly on Prayer* (San Diego: Harcourt Brace Jovanovich, 1963), 102.

49. Ibid., 103.

50. Sayer, *Jack: A Life of C. S. Lewis,* 227.

51. Lewis, *"Dawn Treader,"* p. 16.

52. Ibid., 209.

53. Ibid., 16.

54. Lewis, *Surprised by Joy,* 176.

55. C. S. Lewis, *The Silver Chair* (New York: Collier Books, 1953), 6–7.

56. Ibid.

57. Lewis, *The Magician's Nephew,* 102ff.

58. C. S. Lewis, *The Lion, the Witch and the Wardrobe* (New York: Collier Books, 1950), 159.

59. Ibid., 164ff.

60. Lewis, *The Silver Chair*, 211.

61. C. S. Lewis, *The Last Battle* (New York: Collier Books, 1956), 149–151.

62. Leo Tolstoy, *War and Peace*, in *Great Books of the Western World* (Chicago: Encyclopedia Britannica, Inc., 1952).

63. Lewis, *Surprised by Joy*, 61.

64. Lewis, "The Weight of Glory," in *The Weight of Glory* (Grand Rapids, Mich.: William B. Eerdmans, 1972), 12.

65. Sayer, *Jack: A Life of C. S. Lewis*, 76.

66. Lewis, *Surprised by Joy*, 20.

67. Ibid., 106.

68. C. S. Lewis, "Preface of 1943," in *The Pilgrim's Regress* (Grand Rapids, Mich.: William B. Eerdmans, 1976), 9–10.

69. C. S. Lewis, *A Grief Observed* (New York: Seabury Press, 1961), 42–43.

70. Lewis, *The Magician's Nephew*, 72.

71. Ibid., 18.

72. Lewis, *Prince Caspian*, 163.

73. Lewis, *Mere Christianity*, 120.

74. Ibid., 121.

75. Lewis, *The Last Battle*, 196.

76. John Peterson, "I've a Home Beyond the River," copyright © 1958, Singspiration, Inc.

77. William Morris, *The Well at the World's End* (Berkeley Heights, New Jersey: Wildside Press, 2000), 16.

78. Ibid., 4.

79. Lewis, *Surprised by Joy*, 145.

80. Ibid., 144–145.

81. Lewis, "Sometimes Fairy Stories May Say Best What's to Be Said," in *Of Other Worlds*, 36.

82. Sayer, *Jack: A Life of C. S. Lewis*, 316.

83. Lewis, *Of Other Worlds*, 20.

84. Lewis, *Surprised by Joy*, 66.

85. Ibid., 184.

86. Augustine, *Confessions*, trans. Rex Warner (New York: Mentor Books, 1963), 17.

87. Sayer, *Jack: A Life of C. S. Lewis*, 319.

Bibliography

Augustine, *Confessions,* translated by Rex Warner. New York: Mentor Books, 1963.

The Bruderhof Community, *Behold That Star: A Christmas Anthology.* Rifton, New York: Plough Publishing House, 1966.

Calvin, John. *The Best of John Calvin.* Grand Rapids, Mich.: Baker Book House, 1981.

Chesterton, G. K. *The Everlasting Man.* New York: Image Books, 1955.

———. *Orthodoxy.* New York: Image Books, 1959.

Coleridge, Samuel Taylor. *Samuel Taylor Coleridge: Selected Poems.* New York: Gramercy Books, 1996.

Dorsett, Lyle W. and Marjorie Lamp Mead, eds. *C. S. Lewis: Letters to Children,* New York: Scribner, 1996.

Dostoevsky, Fyodor. *The Brothers Karamazov,* in *Great Books of the Western World.* Chicago: Encyclopedia Britannica, Inc., 1952.

Downing, David. *The Most Reluctant Convert: C. S. Lewis's Journey to Faith.* Downers Grove, Ill.: InterVarsity Press, 2002.

Dunsany, Lord. *The King of Elfland's Daughter.* New York: The Ballantine Publishing Group, 1999.

Lewis, C. S. *The Lion, the Witch and the Wardrobe.* New York: Collier Books, 1950.

———. *Prince Caspian.* New York: Collier Books, 1951.

——. *The Voyage of the "Dawn Treader."* New York: Collier Books, 1952.

——. *The Silver Chair*. New York: Collier Books, 1953.

——.*The Horse and His Boy*. New York: Collier Books, 1954.

——. *The Magician's Nephew*. New York: Collier Books, 1955.

——. *The Last Battle*. New York: Collier Books, 1956.

——. *The Great Divorce*. New York: Simon & Schuster, 1996.

——. *A Grief Observed*. New York: Seabury Press, 1961.

——. *Letters to Malcolm: Chiefly on Prayer*. San Diego: Harcourt Brace Jovanovich, 1963.

——. *Mere Christianity*. New York: Collier Books, 1952.

——. *Miracles*. New York: MacMillan, 1960.

——. *Of Other Worlds,* edited by Walter Hooper. San Diego: Harcourt Brace Jovanovich, 1966.

——. *Out of the Silent Planet*. New York: Macmillan, 1944.

——. *Perelandra*. New York: Macmillan, 1944.

——. *That Hideous Strength*. New York: Macmillan, 1944.

——. *The Pilgrim's Regress*. Grand Rapids, Mich.: William B. Eerdmans, 1976.

——. *Surprised by Joy*. Glasgow: William Collins Sons & Company, 1955.

————. *The Weight of Glory*. Grand Rapids, Mich.: William B. Eerdmans, 1972.

Melville, Herman. *Moby Dick*. New York: Macmillan, 1962.

Morris, William. *The Well at the World's End*. Berkeley Heights, New Jersey: Wildside Press, 2000.

Otto, Rudolf. *The Idea of the Holy*. Oxford, England: Oxford University Press, 1923.

Plato. *Phaedrus,* in *Great Books of the Western World*. Chicago: Encyclopedia Britannica, Inc., 1952.

Pope, Alexander. *The Complete Poetical Works of Alexander Pope*. London: Macmillan and Company, 1885.

Sayer, George. *Jack: A Life of C. S. Lewis*. Wheaton, Ill.: Crossway Books, 1988.

Sibley, Brian and Alison Sage. *A Treasury of Narnia*. London: HarperCollins, 1999.

Thompson, Francis. *The Complete Poetical Works of Francis Thompson*. New York: Boni and Liveright, Inc., 1913.

Tolkien, J. R. R. *The Lord of the Rings*. Boston: Houghton Mifflin Company, 1954.

————. *The Silmarillion*. Boston: Houghton Mifflin Company, 1977.

————. *The Tolkien Reader*. New York: Ballantine Books, 1966.

Tolstoy, Leo. *War and Peace,* in *Great Books of the Western World*. Chicago: Encyclopedia Britannica, Inc., 1952.